"American Christianity at its wor... ...ty coupled with hubristic, macho triur... ...o-tential of Christianity at its best by le... ...re toward healing. For those who ma... ...ra Truax, in her words and in her minis... ...es a pastoral grace that invites us to experience the rawness of an honest story where nothing remains but grace."

Soong-Chan Rah, author of *The Next Evangelicalism*

"As a driven 44-year-old professional living in New York City, I find my Christian faith more and more an oddity in the eyes of my vibrant group of diverse colleagues and friends—like a great ape at the zoo, perfectly fine for observation and amusement, but always to be kept safely behind protective glass. I'm convinced Laura Truax's book is written with me and my friends in mind. She speaks to those of us still working it all out. She reminds us that we've all been undone and points us to the wholeness that can be found in God's unquenchable love."

Rob Acton, executive director, Taproot Foundation, NYC

"True friendship and spiritual growth often begin with brutal honesty and self-awareness. I'd rather be in a faith community where people are real and raw than perfect and fake. If we have the courage to admit it, most of us have been undone by something in our lives. In this book Laura Sumner Truax encourages us to embrace these mistakes, disappointments and difficulties as the place where we begin to discover who we really are as beloved children of God."

Mark Scandrette, author of *Free* and *Practicing the Way of Jesus*

"If I could bequeath a grand title like 'America's Pastor' on a single individual, it would be Laura Truax. This, her first book, is both beautiful and accessible, distinctively Christian and broadly spiritual, and as wise as it is down-to-earth. And at every turn, in the best sense of the word, it is truly pastoral."

Brian D. McLaren, author and speaker (brianmclaren.net)

"Websites and bookshelves are filled with timely, trendy spiritual topics. They offer promises of success, happiness and victorious living. This book is not among them. There is no 'rub-the-Bible-get-three-wishes' piety here. No three-point plan to a better you. Instead, Laura Truax has offered a timeless take on the struggles to live a human life in a universe that is both delightful and destructive. With a candid, straightforward approach, Truax invites us to take an honest inventory about what motivates us, what we value and who, what and how we love. With humor and clarity, Truax presents the classic tenets of the Christian faith in a convincing, if not convicting, fashion. This book will not change your life. But it will lead you to the God who can."

Todd E. Johnson, theological director of the Brehm Center for Worship, Theology and the Arts, **Fuller** Theological Seminary

LAURA
SUMNER TRUAX

WHEN COMING APART PUTS
YOU BACK TOGETHER

IVP Books

An imprint of InterVarsity Press
Downers Grove, Illinois

InterVarsity Press
P.O. Box 1400, Downers Grove, IL 60515-1426
World Wide Web: www.ivpress.com
Email: email@ivpress.com

InterVarsity Press® is the book-publishing division of InterVarsity Christian Fellowship/USA®, a
movement of students and faculty active on campus at hundreds of universities, colleges and schools of
nursing in the United States of America, and a member movement of the International Fellowship of
Evangelical Students. For information about local and regional activities, write Public Relations Dept.,
InterVarsity Christian Fellowship/USA, 6400 Schroeder Rd., P.O. Box 7895, Madison, WI 53707-7895,
or visit the IVCF website at <www.intervarsity.org>.

Scripture quotations, unless otherwise noted, are from the New Revised Standard Version of the Bible,
copyright 1989 by the Division of Christian Education of the National Council of the Churches of
Christ in the USA. Used by permission. All rights reserved.

While all stories in this book are true, some names and identifying information in this book have been
changed to protect the privacy of the individuals involved.

Cover design: Cindy Kiple
Interior design: Beth Hagenberg
Images: © Hande Guleryuz Yuce/iStockphoto

ISBN 978-0-8308-4306-0

Printed in the United States of America ∞

Library of Congress Cataloging-in-Publication Data

Truax, Laura Sumner, 1961-
  Undone : when coming apart puts you back together / Laura Sumner Truax.
    pages cm
  Includes bibliographical references.
  ISBN 978-0-8308-4306-0 (pbk. : alk. paper)
  1. Suffering—Religious aspects—Christianity. I. Title.
  BV4909.T78 2013
  248.8'6—dc23

                                                                    2013007723

P   17   16   15   14   13   12   11   10   9   8   7   6   5   4   3   2   1
Y   27   26   25   24   23   22   21   20   19   18   17   16   15   14   13

Dedicated to the people of

LaSalle Street Church

Contents

1 Coming Undone 9
The Best Worst Day of My Life

Part 1: Excluded by Fear

2 Broken Relationships and the Beginning of Emptiness .   21

3 Wanting More, Finding Less.   34

4 Hiding Behind Masks   45

5 Behind the Mask   60

6 Transforming Fear   74

Part 2: Rediscovering Trust

7 The Risk of Trust   91

8 The Reward of Trust   105

9 What Does God Want from Me?   119

10 Childlike Trust   130

Part 3: Finding Real Connection

11 Restoring Your Identity   149

12 Imagine Love.   163

13 Community.   178
The Third Way

14 Little Choices. 191
    It's All Little Choices

15 The Arc of the Future 200

Acknowledgments 215

Notes 217

Questions for Reflection or Discussion 220

1

Coming Undone

The Best Worst Day of My Life

I had just finished two Sara Lee coffee cakes. Butter streusel. The kind loaded with butter and cinnamon and sugar. Somehow I managed to take them out of the oven at exactly the right moment—when all the little buttery bits of the streusel topping, those little bits that could burn if you left them in too long, were perfectly toasted and brown but still buttery. When I sank my teeth into the cake, it went right down. I ate piece after piece after piece. There are six good-sized pieces in each Sara Lee coffee cake. I ate them all. Twice.

Then I started on a nice big glass of red wine.

It was 2:30 on a hot afternoon in Atlanta, and I sat on my little concrete balcony overlooking the dolled-up retention pond the management company described as a "lake." The cracked tennis courts lay beyond; I watched the hazy steam radiate off the pavement and dissolve into the thick, humid air.

I had just returned from the divorce court where the judge had declared my three-year marriage to be over. It was anticlimactic.

After furious fights, demobilizing depression and estranged disinterest, I expected a pounding gavel and a thundering pronouncement. Instead, a busy and distracted judge glanced at the papers, scribbled his name and mumbled that our marriage was "hereby dissolved."

After briefly meeting the eyes of the man who suddenly was not my husband—what would be our final glance at each other—we left through different exits, saying nothing.

We didn't need to say anything. His look spoke the words he had been saying for months: Our marriage had failed because of me. The commitments I had made and the vows I had given three years ago had lost their meaning. He wasn't the one who felt trapped—it was me. He wasn't the one who was drowning under water—it was me. I was the one who had let him down and shamed his family. I was the one who couldn't keep it going anymore, and by walking away I was the one mocking what marriage was supposed to mean.

His glance at me spoke the anger, the judgment, the bitterness he deserved to hold toward me. His hard expression revealed the hurt I had brought to him and the profound disappointment I had turned out to be.

And he was right. I was the one who was leaving. As he had written into the divorce complaint, he had been willing to continue pursuing counseling, open to having me return as his wife, "interested in my redemption," as he put it. It was me. I wasn't willing.

Looking out over the retention pond, I knew that this was the worst day of my life. What I didn't yet know was that it was also the best day.

The day my divorce was final was the day I was forced to stop pretending. I was never going to be the person who always did the right thing, looked the right way. I wasn't the perky Christian with the seminary-bound husband. I wasn't going to always do good and love children and never utter a cuss word. My voice wasn't always going to be kind when I answered the telephone. My faith wasn't going to be unflappable and my record unvarnished.

I sat there on my little concrete terrace and revisited some of the dark moments of the last three years. Then I started to cry. Hot tears of shame slipped down my cheeks when I thought about all the pious things I had said to others. The many times I firmly said, "Pray and it will work out." I was ashamed at the smug advice, the hackneyed words and silent judgment I had bestowed upon friends who had failed. I remembered the number of times I had pursed my lips at someone's mistakes—*Why can't they just get it together?*

Nope. I had crossed a threshold that meant that I could never go back to that black-and-white world. From that day forward I was going to check the "divorced" box whenever I filled out a survey. I was going to be suspect in some Christian circles, wearing the modern-day "A" as a perpetual sign of my shame.

I had failed. I knew that. My friends knew that. God knew that. And for the first time since I could remember, I didn't have to succeed. No one really expected me to succeed. Hiding and pretending was no longer an option for me. All I could do was say, "Yep. This is who I am."

I Am Undone

Have you ever hit bottom? Have you been cut to the quick by coming face to face with who you *really* are? Have you ever been in that place where you just can't hide?

Maybe you've felt just what I'm talking about. Maybe it was the day of your divorce. Or the morning after that night you'd really rather forget. Maybe it was the day you were picked up by the police or found yourself in an unfamiliar bed. For my friend Vanessa it was when her husband announced he had a pregnant girlfriend. For Nicole it was when the bank foreclosed on her house. And for Jerry it was the day his brother called the family together for an intervention, forcing his drinking into the light. Most of us eventually come to one of those moments when the bottom falls out, and we find that the way we've been living just won't work anymore.

It can feel like the worst day of your life, can't it? But that day—that moment—also has a little spark within it that can ignite something huge. And because of that spark, that worst day carries with it the potential to be best day of your life.

I didn't know all that failure was going to teach me. There's no way I could have known it on that day when I coated my insides with butter and wine. There's no way I could have known how liberating failure was going to be.

Failure ripped the mask off my craving for perfection; it exposed to me the real me. What I saw wasn't pretty, it wasn't holy and it wasn't good. But it was real. And in exposing what was real, failure awakened me to all that had been fake and futile. Not the stuff out there, but the stuff inside. In me.

A very long time ago a man known only as Isaiah found himself with his mask stripped away. He got a glimpse of another world—one that was inhabited by beings good and holy and true. He faced the chasm between that world and the impoverished state of his own soul. He confronted the aching hunger of his existence, and he gasped, "Woe is me! for I am *undone*" (Isaiah 6:5 KJV). Literally the word in the original Hebrew means "I have ceased, I am destroyed. My old self no longer exists." This is what being "undone" does: It destroys the old. The old patterns, the former lies, the worn-out stories. They simply fail.

This book is for everyone who has felt the wincing wound of failure. Not just a setback; a setback still allows you to saddle up again and ride back out. But failure leaves you standing still. Failure can show you to yourself in a way that is unmistakably real. It gives you no place to hide and no rock to crawl under. Failure can leave you standing in the middle of the field during a lightning storm. Exposed and vulnerable.

That is, if you're lucky.

I was lucky. Though luck in the traditional sense had little to do with it. I was *graced*—to use a term I'm more comfortable with. When I was exposed, divine grace smiled on me and allowed me to unflinchingly see . . . me. When failure confronted me with who I was, it also confronted me with who I could be. I didn't know it then, but that meant everything, and it was the door to everything good that was to follow.

I was undone.

Maybe you are where I was. After you've disappointed and failed those who hoped in you—once you've failed yourself and failed whomever or whatever you hold God to be—then there's not much else you can do to ingratiate yourself. You've been stripped to the core. The pretenses have fallen away, and you stand unadorned and undiluted.

Jesus would say rejoice and be glad. Because he knew that these days of failure are the days when new people are made and new lives begin. It wasn't a given; he knew that better than anyone. But it was a possibility. Again and again, Jesus awakened people to the possibility of the present failure. Calling them to recognize that failure and weakness are precisely the elements God uses.

Some people recognized what he was saying. Some people even embraced what he was teaching, and a small few began living what he was claiming. They were tired of living a charade and suffocating under their masks. They decided to just come clean and accept whatever consequences and chaos may follow.

This is a story about what happened to them. This is a story about what happened to me. And this might be the story about what could happen to you.

Beginning the Journey

The worst day didn't become the best day overnight, of course. It took years for me to begin to recognize crushing failure as being anything but, well, crushing. It took years longer to see the implications of living without my safety blankets, my power trips and my pretty masks. And it took even longer before I could begin to see the whole thing as freedom.

But the Christian texts consistently revealed the next step and the step after that. The record of Jesus himself pushed me to desire the way of living that he so expertly knew. Jesus was honest; I wanted to be honest. Jesus was loving; I wanted to be loving. Jesus was courageous; I wanted to be courageous. Jesus was free; I wanted—more than anything—to be free. Jesus seemed to inspire the people he encountered, one after the other, to climb out of fear and isolation into courage and community. They put down their habits of duplicity and deception, and they started telling the truth. I hoped that their story could be mine as well.

Perhaps that's your journey too, and maybe you're wondering if you can find some way to know love and honesty and courage and freedom. This isn't an answer book. It would be great if I could distill what I've learned into the ABCs of it all. I wish I could tell you exactly what to do in your very particular situation at this moment. But I can't tell you, and God likely won't tell you. I had to release my grip on that myth, and you do too if you're going to inch closer toward the reality of what is—and the promise of what could be.

It took me a long time to diagnose what was going on in me, and even longer, of course, to figure out why. But the root cause was really pretty simple: I was afraid. My fear didn't manifest itself like the paranoia of people who see danger everywhere, or like the timidity of those who stand motionless because they're afraid of taking the wrong next step. No, my fear was blanketed in working hard, in being a team player, and in a particular expression of religiosity that looked like kindness, openness and vulnerability—except it was really pride, power and self-containment. I would say the right words to comfort people even while thinking within myself, *Quit bellyaching!* Or I'd cover my insecurities by giving the answer people around me wanted to hear, instead of revealing what I was really thinking or feeling. It took me a while to realize it all stemmed from a deeper sense of fear.

Fear is a funny thing. Where I grew up in central Florida, we feared hurricanes, cold snaps capable of freezing the orange groves, and the growing influx of folks from the north. In other words, fear was generally directed to these external threats that we could do little to prevent. Fear, in this sense, is an expression of not being able to control outside forces.

These fears are real. No doubt about it. But I've found that the more insidious fears—the ones I actually operate under—are the fears that come from internal threats. My first real expression of fear became real to me when I realized how much I feared being different. Individual. Unique. And just as much as I feared being different, I feared being irrelevant. If I didn't bring some value to somebody, then who would want to be around me? In some ways, this was so much worse than the fear of a hurricane. There's no escaping the fear of who you really might be.

I quickly learned how to bring value. I learned to make other people feel good about themselves. I became an excellent chameleon. A chameleon is one of the more common lizards in Florida. They can be challenging to spot because within minutes of entering a new terrain, their skin changes into the color of the background they stand against. The substance just underneath a chameleon's skin operates as a camouflage by reflecting the various color pigments surrounding the lizard. The substance itself has no color.

Maybe you wince to compare yourself to a lizard, but imagine how protected you are when you can blend in so well to your environment that you don't need additional defenses.

That was me.

I could move comfortably from my family setting to my church setting just by changing my locale, blending in and pretending.

We play the game of being somebody we're not.

The chameleon is the person in us who doesn't want to reveal the truth about who we are or what we have done—or what we are thinking we are going to do as soon as we can. The pretender is the one who can't resist giving a fact if she knows it and looking important if he can manage it. The fearful one is Adam or Eve in the garden, determined to cover up what they've done, doing their best to hide and worried that they can't keep hiding forever.

To paraphrase T. S. Eliot, many of us rise each morning and put on a face to meet the faces we meet.[1] I got tired of putting on a face each morning to cover over the fears that were swirling inside of me. If you're tired of putting on a face too, then you might want to try doing things another way. The way won't be perfect, it won't be without pain, but it will be real. And real is a really good place to start.

So what's the real story about what happens to people in their worst moments? What really became of those men and women throughout the Scriptures—ancient stories—who hit bottom? What determined whether they made it through dark days and even worse decisions? What happens to people like them and like me? People who are liars and deceivers, fakes and phonies. People who had used others to get what they wanted and lusted after what they didn't have, and always, always, always had this sense that they were created for something different and something better.

What happens to people like us when we begin to see who we are and who we could become? It's a long process. Though my divorce is now more than two decades behind me, the patterns of trying to hide, defend and deceive still creep up on me. They are the shrouded passengers in the back seat. But what I see more clearly and feel more distinctly are the moments of deep joy, the confidence of honesty, the warmth of connectedness. Like Isaiah and those who came before me, I've realized it's all worth it. That the reality of being undone is worth it. Along with the accompanying pain of rejection, the ache of vulnerability, the embarrassment of making public what you once hid—it was all worth it. This is our story.

Part One

Excluded by Fear

2

Broken Relationships and the Beginning of Emptiness

When did my marriage start to fray? I have had some time to think about it now. Since I wasn't using my meager energy to fire a retaliatory attack, and I didn't need to keep holding up my defensive mask, I slowly became aware that I had time to simply analyze and reflect.

And did I ever analyze and reflect.

We didn't start out the way we ended up. He didn't start out as selfish and judgmental as he was on that day he left the courthouse. And (while I know it's debatable) I didn't start out as a complaining shrew. No. Neither of us began our relationship that way. We began fresh and full of promise. We were living in uncharted territory, and the land of opportunity stretched as far as our twenty-two-year-old eyes could see.

We could live anywhere! We could do anything! We believed that God himself had brought us together and that the universe herself smiled benignly on our love and our future.

Yet within months after the eager "I do!" I found myself returning to a refrain I didn't dare speak: *Is this it? Is this my life? How did I end up in this place with this person? What went wrong?*

My then-husband, Nigel, and I would get up early each morning to do our daily prayers and Bible study. Sometimes I would be tired from the night before—but fatigue wasn't an excuse to not do what you knew was right—so I would dutifully turn off the alarm, turn on the light and prop my Bible in front of my knees to sit in bed reading. (Nigel told me I should hit the Bible before my feet hit the floor. Oh joy.) Within months I grew to hate this morning discipline. It's not that I didn't want to pray or read—it was the autocratic demand that I must that stung me. Six months into my first marriage I was still getting up early—the Bible was still propped in front of my lap, the black edges still visible above my knee caps. But just beneath the thick edge, hidden from anyone else but me, was the latest issue of *Glamour* magazine. Deceit was creeping in around all the edges of my life.

I tried to go back to the beginning and untangle some of the strands. Yes, yes, every story has a beginning. But this time around, I started to see the unraveling of my marriage as another chapter in an earlier story. It wasn't only my marriage that seemed so unhappy; unhappiness and unfulfillment was everywhere. Our stories all seemed to be part of a story people had begun writing a long time before me.

Frayed

In the beginning . . . God. For the first time in a long time I began really reading the book of Genesis. That first book gives us a record of people who also wondered, *Why am I not happy? What went wrong?*

I have a lot of friends who write off the book of Genesis pretty quickly. (*Adam and Eve . . . really? Come on.*)

They squirm through the details of the Hebrew creation story, reflexively comparing it to what's been learned about the Ice Age, the

Neanderthals, the fossil records and the like. Perhaps this is where Genesis stops for many of us. Right there with our rational questions. We readily spot the things that don't make sense or the descriptions that don't match up with scientific conclusions. (*So you're telling me the earth is only six thousand years old, and we all descended from two people who knew a talking snake?*) And then we simply close the book.

The writers of the Hebrew creation story would have laughed. They were never interested in the questions we now ask of the text. The Hebrews weren't interested in *technique*; they were interested in the *meaning* behind it all. These were the stories they told about themselves. They framed an ethic and a worldview. These were stories that helped explain why brothers had a hard time getting along, why men and women were different from the animals around them. They explored the unseen connectedness of everything that lives. Most importantly, these stories expressed meaning and purpose for humanity.

In the wealth of Near Eastern creation stories, the account of the Hebrews stands out as different. Most creation stories from that period are fraught with high drama. Multiple gods fight among themselves for domination. Gods feel threatened by the world and worried they might lose their power. The relationship between gods and humans is one of animosity as each strives for victory. In contrast, the Hebrew creation story is stark and unadorned. There are no thundering wars, no struggles between rivals, no real turmoil. It's extraordinary in its austerity. The writers portray a creation with just one determined God, resolved to make a garden and longing for companionship. The God of the Hebrews had nothing to fear from humanity; their God was never in competition with this world being created. While other peoples struggled to understand what it was that displeased their gods, the Hebrews understood that God had created intentionally, with purpose and clarity.

All things existed in relationship to each other. The rhythm of the language, the ordered deliberateness of the text, the careful positioning of man and nature, connected and mutually dependent, all point to oneness—a wholeness—that was meant to be. *In the beginning* is describing a home.

And key to this oneness was the tethered relationship of men and women to themselves, to the earth around them and to their Creator.

Annie Dillard, reflecting on the array of species of frogs, says, "Our creator loves pizzazz!"[1] The Hebrews would have resonated with that sentiment. Everything that has been created was created good. You and me included. That goodness never goes away, but soon after creation it sure begins to fray. We quickly come undone. This is what the Hebrews understood too.

The earliest stories they told were of wholeness and fraying edges, of complete goodness and encroaching danger, of an ordered rhythm and a disturbing atonality. Genesis had to do with the human experience—with meaning, love and relationship present all around us.

Still good—but now fraying.

It's that threadbare state that we now endure. The fraying between my ex and me started long before that day in the judge's chambers. It started before the final fights and stony silence. The fabric of our happy home began to come apart early on. *Was it even on our honeymoon?* I wondered. When I wanted to spend a few extra dollars on a photo from the Pirates of the Caribbean ride and he said no? Was it when I scraped the price tag off the fancy mustard I had bought to avoid a judgmental word? It was through those little moments that deceit started to become a way of life for me. I began avoiding the little disagreements, and I realized after a few years I began avoiding a lot of other things.

Just like the story in Genesis, it came unraveled slowly. A favorite poet, Scott Cairns, interprets the Genesis event through this lens of almost imperceptible fraying:

Yes, there was a tree, and upon it, among the wax leaves, an order of fruit which hung plentifully, glazed with dew of a given morning. And there had been some talk off and on—nothing specific—about forgiving the inclination to eat of it. But sin had very little to do with this or with any outright prohibition.

For sin had made its entrance long before the serpent spoke, long before the woman and the man had set their teeth to the pale, stringy flesh, which was, it turns out, also quite without flavor. Rather, sin had come in the midst of an evening stroll, when the woman had reached to take the man's hand and he withheld it.

In this way, the beginning of our trouble came to the garden almost without notice. And in later days, as the man and the woman wandered idly about their paradise, as they continued to enjoy the sensual pleasures of food and drink and spirited coupling even as they sat marveling at the approach of evening and the more lush approach of sleep, they found within themselves a developing habit of resistance.

One supposes that, even then, this new taste for turning away might have been overcome, but that is assuming the two had found the result unpleasant. The beginning of loss was this: Every time some manner of beauty was offered and declined, the subsequent isolation each conceived was irresistible.[2]

This was my life. Exactly. We didn't find turning away from each other to be "unpleasant." Instead, I began to relish the overnight stints Nigel worked as a security guard. It meant less time together—more time for just me. And likewise, when "some manner of beauty was offered" often from one of us who had roused ourselves to an apology of sorts, the other typically and politely declined.

Looking for Home

Years after my divorce, now with a new husband and a new life in a new city, I had a profound experience of what home can mean. Our first home (and the one we still live in) was badly in need of a paint job. Being a hundred-year-old wooden house, it needed more than just a few gallons of color. We hired a team of guys who probably underbid the job and underestimated the work.

The project dragged on and on as the crew chief kept reducing his staff one by one, transferring them to more lucrative jobs. As early spring moved into mid-summer, I decided to get more involved by pitching in and helping them by sanding and scraping. The fullness of time found me one late July afternoon, high on a ladder outside our second floor window, seething and scraping away, shoulder to shoulder with one of the painters—one of the men actually paid to do the job.

Since, in my mind, I was working on Sunday's sermon just days away, I turned to Pete the Painter and explained my text for Sunday. I asked him, "What do you think of when you hear the word *Eden?*" Without a pause, Pete replied, "It makes me want to go home."

Eden. Home.

Now maybe I just had a particularly erudite house painter, or maybe there just is a common consciousness that Eden connotes for many of us. "Home is the place where, when you have to go there, they have to take you in," Robert Frost wrote.[3] I've always liked the stability of that quote, but I chafed at the resigned responsibility I heard in it. Isn't there a place that wants to take us in—not only because we're family but because we're just so . . . *wanted?*

Growing up, home for me had been the place where I had to measure up and was generally found lacking. My brothers and sister all seemed to work harder, show more initiative, exude more confidence and simply succeed more than I did. My divorce made me realize I had never been at home in a place where I could relax and know that I was wanted no matter what I did, I was loved no matter how I acted, and I was okay regardless of how I felt about myself.

In the Genesis story we first see the fraying of relationships in the well-known encounter under that tree in the garden. The woman, Eve, starts to doubt the credibility of what she had known up to this point. Was there really an interconnectedness within it all? Were there really relationships of trust and mutual dependency? Could this divine interplay among men, women and God be counted on?

When the serpent poses the question to Eve, it's not a simple question. He twists it. It's not a yes-no question. It's a question that forces Eve to stand and reflect—*Did God really say, "You can't eat of any tree in the garden?"*

You know the deck is stacked against Eve here. And us too, right? Eve's not playing with a full hand of knowledge. In fact, Eve never even heard the command in the first place. Eve got it from Adam. He's the only one who heard God's commandment (see Genesis 2:15-17; 3:1-4).

So when Eve (in sort-of-knowledge, sort-of-ignorance) responds to the temptation at hand—to the serpent at hand—she doesn't even have all the facts. She's responding based on what she thinks she might remember from Adam telling her this. And she doesn't remember it right. She responds to him, "Well, we can't eat *or even touch* the tree that's found in the middle of the garden."

This isn't just semantics here. This little nugget of the story stayed alive for hundreds of years before it was ever written down. There's something really important that the early Israelites saw here.

We can't eat or even touch.

One rabbi says that when the serpent heard the claim that death would follow anyone who touched the tree, the serpent promptly wrapped himself around the tree and shook it with all of his might, and all the fruit fell down to the ground. *Death? Really? You can see with your own eyes that I am still alive.*

There's something that happens when the credibility of what we think we know is undermined. She *thought* that's what Adam said.

But she didn't quite know, and that uncertainty made it all start to come unraveled. It was the beginning of her undoing.

What Eve is wondering about are the same questions we wonder about as well. Can we really count on others to come through in the way we need them to come through? Can we honestly depend on the supposition that there is a deep and eternal rhythm that unites all? And perhaps most pressingly, can we trust there is a divine presence, an interested Creator who initiates and perhaps *even desires* a relationship with us? It's at her home, where she should have felt at ease, that doubt and mistrust step in to undermine Eve's confidence. It seems all it takes for her to begin doubting the security of home is a little twisting of the words, a few additions here and a few deletions there.

Sometimes, for me, it doesn't even take that much. I can feel wronged by the smallest of expressions, the weakest of words. I can mentally construct entire conversations from a glance. And when someone doesn't respond the way I imagined they should or would, I can easily believe that we are estranged, alienated, even though I have no reason beyond a shrug for suspecting that.

You may have similar tendencies. This is what it's like when we don't really live at home. This is what happens when we forget that we can trust the goodness of right now, when we forget that we can depend on Someone who desires us. This is how we live when we don't believe that the door to divine presence is open for us. We can't see that not only is the door open but the porch light is on as well.

East of Eden

When the Hebrews talked about sin, they were talking about separation. Separation comes in a number of flavors. The Hebrews had at least three words to describe different aspects of sin.[4] First is the separation we are most familiar with. The Hebrew word is ʿāwāh. This is the word for the lies we tell, for the vows we break, for the gossip we spread and for the honor we steal. *ʿĀwāh* describes our wrong actions, our bad behavior and our even worse thoughts. This is the alienation we can describe, measure and count. We can dole out punishments and seek clear retribution for many of our *ʿāwāh* deeds. *ʿĀwāh* is the starting point for the closeted room of the confessional: "Forgive me, father, for I have sinned."

Whenever someone is talking about sin, *ʿāwāh* is generally the only framework they have—it's simple and concrete. The problem is that it doesn't give words to my deeper attitudes, my frayed hope, my ambitions—both grandiose and paltry.

The word the Hebrews used for this deeper condition is *ḥāṭāh*. I've heard it described as missing the mark, but it's more helpful for me to describe it as the risks I don't take, the self that seems beyond my grasp or the hopes that seem too lofty to fulfill. One way of thinking about it is the quote by Marianne Williamson: "Our deepest fear is not that we are inadequate. Our deepest fear is that we are powerful beyond imagination."[5]

Ḥāṭāh describes all the ways we draw back when we should be moving forward. *Ḥāṭāh* is that pull of fear that stops us from loving because we may not be loved in return; and always it's that aching cavern that opens in our hearts when we realize we are not the person we longed to be or hoped we'd be.

This is also *ḥāṭāh*: We fully expected to be one kind of person and instead we've been blown off course. One of the clearest examples is found in the story of Samson. Samson is a classic sort of literary figure—a strong man of rippling muscles and heroic courage—oversized stories and an oversized ego. Samson was undone by the beautiful Delilah, the woman who cuts off his hair—the secret to his strength—and gives him over to the Philistines. But Samson did a lot of living before he ever met Delilah. She was just one of the last in a long series of questionable choices Samson made. Samson was a man who had everything needed to be great and to play a central role in the future of Israel.

But he got seriously sidetracked. Samson was a man of great passions. He loved power and he loved wielding it. He loved sex and he loved having sex with women. He is a poster child of a man who never needed to say *no*. What he wanted, he got. What he saw, he took. What he hungered for, he ate.

It didn't start out this way. It started out so well. Awesome, really. There are angelic pronouncements at his birth. It's a miracle! The angels tell a barren woman she is going to have a son. The boy will be special, set apart, for he's going to deliver Israel from his enemies.

How cool is that? To know you are blessed by God?

Maybe you have felt before that sense of mission: *I was meant for something special. I may have a purpose.* This is what Samson had, but his inability to say no to the experiences that brought him short-term satisfaction left him blind to the opportunities to say yes to real greatness. Samson was destined for greatness, but it didn't turn out that way (see Judges 13:1–16:31).

Samson's greatest gifts had a shadow side to them. His greatest attribute had a powerful underside that threatened to destroy him. Samson's potential for greatness was in the power of his body, and his fatal flaw was in the way he used it. His raging testosterone brought illustrious military conquests, but how was he to apply that overabundance of "manly" energy to his everyday life? He didn't know how to integrate the gift into his normal life. Thus Samson turned his prodigious military conquests to sexual conquests and macho one-upmanship. In situation after situation Samson was either thinking about sex, having sex or facing the consequences of sex. From prostitutes to standing up a bride at the altar. From living with one woman in Gaza to falling in love with the infamous Delilah. Sex and violent power were all over his life.

The arc of Samson's life is his drive to satisfy his passions. Even if it kills him.

How does Samson go from this little miracle baby to this man of voracious appetites who gives us one of the most hedonistic portrayals in the entire Bible? Probably in much the same way we do. We create our lives with little choices. Things that seem of almost no consequence. No different from Samson, really.

Samson had a series of places where he could have used his power for good—but he chose otherwise. A series of little choices. To defy his parents. To break a promise. To take without thinking of the impact of his selfishness. To take revenge.

Again and again the Samson cycle revolves around having his needs for importance, recognition and pleasure met. He lost sight of the person he could have been over a series of little choices—the same choices we face.

Ḥāṭāh points out how dangerous it is to not tell yourself no. Samson was a man who couldn't say no. Who needn't say no. His power and his prestige allowed him that.

And in this way Samson seems a lot like us. Over time, this inability to say no eats away at us in a way we can't even see. We cease to imagine what we might have been. What we might have wanted, even what we were originally aiming for in the first place. Samson ended up, as the poet John Milton put it, "eyeless in Gaza," unable to even see what held him captive.[6] But as it tends to be with us, it wasn't the Philistines who really blinded him, it was ḥāṭāh.

Ḥāṭāh keeps *People* magazine in business. We can read about how some actor's risk-taking nature was necessary in his or her work but untamed in the actor's relationships, that same quality strangled any hope for stability. Ḥāṭāh is what we see in the political or religious figure who achieves greatness in leadership but squanders his or her powers for persuasion on a cheap thrill in a backwater motel.

ʿĀwāh describes those deliberate actions we do when we are not at home—those actions that separate us from each other. Ḥāṭāh gives voice to that angst and longing that separate us from ourselves. But the Hebrews had one more word that revealed the ultimate undoing of the whole system: *pāšaʿ*.

Pāšaʿ is the word for all of life that is lived east of Eden now. It's the growing crack that separates us from our water systems and the rain forests. It's the break of alienation that allows us to read about rivers running red with blood in Central Africa, outbreaks of malaria in Ethiopia, ethnic cleansing in Southern Europe. It's all right there in the news, but we can only bear to glance at it. Then we turn away. We put down the newspaper, change the channel, close the browser. We retreat back into the dark, into *pāšaʿ*.

Pāšaʿ affirms we live in a world far larger than ourselves whose systems are beyond our individual actions. We may be separated from the outcomes, unable to explicitly see the connection between our smart phones and human rights abuses among the mining companies that provide the titanium for those phones. We may know only vague rumors of blood diamonds or sweatshop clothing. We may not directly support these systems. Yet still—somewhere in this matrix, *pāšaʿ* demands we still bear some responsibility to make things right again. *Pāšaʿ* describes structures that need to be fixed, and it doesn't let us off the hook just because we aren't directly keeping these oppressive wrongs in place.

Eve forgot she lived at home with people who loved her. And when she forgot, she first mistrusted the One who created her and knew her best. Instead of defining herself by trusting that home itself could be trusted, fear led her to believe she could really only rely on herself. Fear led her to withdraw in silence. It's *ʿāwāh* when she takes the fruit into her hands and its flesh into her mouth. And soon it's *ḥāṭāh* as her husband uses her as a scapegoat. No longer is their relationship grounded in the kind of mutuality that had first nurtured it. Leaving home meant sharp elbows and a me-first mentality. That mentality was necessary for this archetypal couple who could no longer trust the love between them.

As they pick up their tools to work the earth for food and begin killing the animals for their clothing, they know the weight of *pāšaʿ* all too well. The open door is no longer visible. The porch light is now replaced by a nomad's torch of fire. Our ancestors go out—and you and I go out—to find some semblance of home in a world altogether too chilly and inhospitable.

When I began to feel the separation growing between my ex-husband and me, I initially tried to make sense of it all by starting right where we were. As if we were two people who started from scratch. But we weren't starting from scratch. Each of us dragged our old stories into our marriage. I hauled my feelings of inadequacy and judgment. I would work long and hard to overcome my inadequacies. He carried his long-held attitudes of superiority and triumph. He would do whatever it took to succeed. As individuals these stories had worked for us.

This is the full weight of sin—of separation—a weight we pass down through our families and our culture from generation to generation. Along with the remorse, the discouragement and the if-onlys. Eve and Adam are left wanting more and finding less at every step of the journey. Distrust and disinterest tracked them the same way they tracked my ex-husband and me. Never really confident of each other's love, never really sure that the other had our back. And always—always—wanting to find how to get home. To that place where someone would welcome us just as we are and open the door wide to receive us, even in our dusty traveling clothes and carrying everything we own.

3

Wanting More,
Finding Less

A long way from home. That's where I found myself. Undone and excluded. Sometimes we feel the separation as a malaise in our gut. Angst and longing provide clues that we are not all right. We know there should be something more in our relationships, in our work, in our aspirations—but what is it? How do we know what we're looking for? And where on earth would we ever find it?

My ex and I looked for that satisfaction in religious piety. In doing the right things, knowing the right answers. Surely the path home would be apparent to those trying to do right, we thought. Most everyone in our small circle of devout Christian friends were trying to get home by the same path. We held each other accountable to study hard and pray even harder. We kept careful prayer journals; we memorized Scripture verses. (Oy! The shoeboxes full of well-worn memorized index cards.) All these practices—that started out so well intentioned—became just another kind of mask for me.

How could I reveal to my prayer group that I hid a *Glamour* magazine behind my Bible? How could I tell my earnest girlfriends that sometimes I just stopped eating for days because I could feel myself fraying on the inside?

Religious fervor was one way of trying to find home. Others of us—maybe most of us—are looking for the way home through the narrative of twenty-first-century American life. That's a pretty good place to start because we know it so well. On our best days the path toward home is marked by responsible living, by diligent work and saving, and by constructive goals and rewards. On our worst days we stumble down a path of worry, grasping and some amount of greed and self-indulgence. We navigate between the rewards we expect and the satisfaction we demand.

Unsatisfied

Finding our way home through accumulation and acquisition is a well worn road. If we're walking on it, we certainly follow in some pretty big footprints. Religious leaders throughout the ages have wrestled with it, including Jesus of Nazareth. In one of the most well-known stories in the New Testament, an anxious man approaches Jesus with a vital question.

The scene takes place near the end of Jesus' public ministry. Things are coming to a close. The tent revival is folding up; Jesus is leaving town, soon to hoist a cross on his back. Meanwhile, one man stands in the back, waiting for the roadies to move away so he could have just a moment to ask the question that's been eating away at him. He hangs around, lingering until the moment is almost lost. The traveling evangelist has picked up his stuff and turned away, leaving for the next town, when finally the nameless man springs into action, running after Jesus and yelling, Wait! Wait!

As the writer Mark says it, the man fell to his knees before Jesus and asked him, "Good Teacher, what must I do to inherit eternal life?" (Mark 10:17-22).

What? Eternal life? you ask. I'm just trying to find a little satisfaction right now.

Well, so was he. "Eternal life" was a mode of expressing the same things we seek too. Please, can you tell me how I can have just a little peace in my heart? Can you tell me how I can wake up in the morning at ease with what the day will bring? Can you tell me how I can trust others and stop protecting myself at every turn? Please! For the love of God, can you tell me how I can get home again?

The man is seeking the good life—the same life you and I want. And he thought he was doing the right things to get the good life. He's not squandered his years so far. He's responsible, faithful. He's a respectable man. No wild living for him. He speaks with civil words, tries to give honest answers. He respects his mother; he loves his father. No doubt, he is well regarded and much envied in his community.

But there is something missing. And although it's not seen on the outside, he knows it. The young man feels it. Something's killing him. Robbing him of the kind of peace and vibrancy that he thought would be his. When he sees Jesus, he sees something that makes him think this teacher might have the answer—the solution to this gnawing malaise.

Something's not right, Jesus! Something is sucking the life out of me. What do I do to have the kind of life I really want to have?

Ten Percent More Happiness

This is where our prevailing narrative of American life breaks down. We don't find our way back home just by following the expectations of those around us.

Even the hard-working, responsible pursuit of a good job, a good home and the pleasures of life are not enough in themselves to answer our angst. In survey after survey, when people are asked how much money they need to be happy or secure—the answer is consistently, "I just need 10 percent more." This response is the same across all income levels. No matter whether our income is $50,000 or $250,000, regardless of whether we're making upwards of half a million or living a hair above the poverty line, we all need just 10 percent more. And no matter how many times we may get that 10 percent more, we don't seem to notice that it doesn't do what we thought it would. We keep following that next 10 percent until we are completely undone—in a mountain of debt and as uneasy as we were when we started.

I feel like I know this Acquisition Road very well. My first husband was studying in seminary; we often thought our marital woes would go away when we made just a little bit more money. When I married my second husband, he was studying in law school. Different profession, different income potential, different everything. Except we found ourselves asking what would we do if we had 10 *percent more?*

Just like my first faith community couldn't help me distinguish between piety and faithfulness, it was challenging to find a church that pointed us to the right path regarding money. The Bible itself presents some conflicting examples of accumulation and wealth. At times the Hebrews sound like they expected the way back home to be paved with concrete rewards.

Early on, the Old Testament shows that a blessed man is often a rich one. For hundreds of years, when the Hebrews told their stories, they were sure to remember that their patriarch Abraham was "very rich in livestock, in silver, and in gold" (Genesis 13:2); that his son Isaac was so wealthy, he was envied by his enemies (see Genesis 24–25); that the wealth of Solomon was so vast that it deserved to be noted in detail—so much detail that entire chapters of the book of Kings read like a balance sheet.

So it shouldn't be surprising that we can think the jig is up when something happens to derail our acquisitions. That is part of the tragedy with the sad story of Job. The first clue his friends have that he's on God's bad side is when his cattle and livestock are lost.

If the accumulation of wealth is a sign of God's blessing, then very naturally we assume that more of it just may be a sign of our increasing favor. If four cows are good, forty are even better!

The institutional church has long been comfortable with wealth. From the jaw-dropping expanse of St. Peter's Basilica in Rome, with its priceless art collection, to the massive modern cathedrals—crystal, stone and glass—along with the small college campus-size worship centers, the Christian church has bedecked itself in the best money can buy.

Today, plenty of Christian leaders teach that God is in the business of blessing our financial life. The November 2009 cover of *The Atlantic* went so far as to suggest that evangelical Christians played a key role in the 2008 housing crash as folks, on the advice of their ministers, stretched to buy bigger houses, because *Didn't God want his people to live the good life?*

One of the only things we know about the questioner in the book of Mark is that he was probably like many of us. He had enough resources to be worried about losing them. He had spent enough of his precious time and energy to acquire things that meant a lot to him, likely working for them with the same hopes and dreams we have as we work for our goods as well. Thinking that the next raise, the next promotion will be just the ticket.

Jesus knows this path is never going to lead us home. And he knows we are going to keep driving down that road until we may not be able to turn around.

Mark said, when Jesus heard the question he looked at the young man and loved him. And maybe Jesus leaned in and looked at him hard and spoke with the greatest of tenderness, thinking, *You are slowly being strangled. Gently and relentlessly, the line is being pulled taut around your neck. And you don't even see it happening.*

Jesus' response to the young man is quick and unflinching. "You want eternal life? Then go and sell all you have."

When Jesus talks about money, he sweats like an evangelist under the floodlights because he knows what's at stake. He knows just how alluring this path looks, and he doesn't miss an opportunity to denounce what he sees going on:

Woe to you who are rich!

You cannot serve God and wealth!

Do not store up . . . treasures.

It is easier for a camel to go through the eye of a needle than for someone who is rich to enter the kingdom of God.

Give to everyone who begs from you!

Sell what you own!

"You fool!" he said to the man building the bigger house—to hold his bigger collection of stuff—to quell the bigger fear: "Tonight your soul is required."[1]

He knows we will always want just 10 percent more.

The Stuff of Fear

It seems the more anxious we are, the more attached we become to some concrete form of home. (Since we can't fabricate a return to Eden, the place of abundance and security, we cling tightly to the smaller places of security and "blessings" we do have.)

We think our relationships may be shaky, so we hold on tighter; we suspect a colleague is doing an end run around us, so we do one first; our children expect a sibling is going to tell on them, so they spill the beans on their brother first. And in so doing, *we set in motion the very things we fear.*

We can do the same thing with our resources as well. There is a great story about this sort of thing throughout the Old Testament book of Exodus. For more than three hundred years, the Hebrews had been in slavery; they were the labor used to build the pyramids of Egypt. Many generations lived and died in numbing conditions.

Then suddenly, through a series of amazing events, the people find themselves freed and immediately rush into the desert to try to find their way home.

But along the way their anxiety elevates beyond control. Freedom begins to look just as bad as slavery did. They bicker and they complain to anyone who will listen about how unfair it all is. They challenge the man who led them out. *Why did you bring us here? Didn't you know we were going to die here? Nobody knows how to get back home!*

And in a move that sounds a lot like Jesus' response to the unidentified questioner, God offers them a way out of their anxiety. He provides food, but food with a caveat. Manna with a memo: *Here it is,* he says. *There is plenty for everyone and for every day, provided you don't take more than you need and you don't try to accumulate it.*

But they were afraid, and being afraid, they were determined to cling to every crumb. This is the Myth of Scarcity—when our anxieties tell us we don't have enough, no matter how much we have. When the Hebrews tried to hold onto the manna gift, it rotted and became filled with maggots. That's so much more expressive—so much more vivid—than what we see when we're buying the new boat or squeezing our new purchases into our burgeoning closets. Our good-life narrative doesn't tell us what the Hebrews could see (and smell) so well as they sat with their rotting manna. Our stuff-blessing culture doesn't reveal to us what Jesus saw so clearly as he watched a beautifully robed rich man wearing an invisible noose.

The reality is, we get sick when we believe God's love is always tied to stuff, and we get sick when satisfying our deepest longings is tied to getting even more stuff.

It will never be enough because we will always seek that 10 percent more. No matter how little or how much we make. No matter how many kids we're paying tuition for or how deeply in debt we are, *If only we made a little bit more, then we would breathe easier.* And we will never know the deep love of God (or the security of Eden) as long as we look for it in what kind of home we live in or what job we do or what car we drive.

This is what Jesus knew. He knew that it was all so consuming and seductive. He knew the path could look beautiful. But he knew it would never lead back home.

A free heart, that's what Jesus was offering the young man. A heart liberated from all the lies and the fears that had been keeping him up at night. But to get this freedom, the man would first have to let go of all the lies he told himself. Like the message that said, *If I only had 10 percent more.*

For him, liberty could begin when he relinquished what he had.

There are several ways Jesus moved people onto the path toward home. He connected people with the poor: *You need each other.* He taught and lived a conscious awareness that God's resources were open to all and never to be hoarded or accumulated. He modeled a life of community, where even the simplest urges of generosity, such as that of a young boy sharing his lunch, could be used to bless thousands of people (see John 6:5-15). And always, Jesus said the way back home was marked by the same explosion of liberating freedom that the Hebrews experienced. You just had to know where to start.

What We Want

For the earnest questioner Jesus began by showing him what the man loved the most. As I sought to learn from the mistakes of my first marriage I became very attuned to the warning signs of false attachments in my second marriage. I wanted to be real about the desires of my heart. I soon realized that I had comfortably replaced the temptations of piety with the desires of consumerism.

Not long ago my husband Terry and I celebrated our twenty-fifth wedding anniversary. Terry and I had been married for twenty years before I ever had a diamond wedding ring on my finger. Twenty years.

Now there are several reasons why we didn't get a ring earlier. Initially my husband and I were both in graduate school. We could barely afford our rent. After that, paying off our student loans became the priority. Around the five-year mark, we really needed a washer and dryer. You know how it goes.

But from year six on we intermittently had the resources to buy a diamond. Even so, we didn't buy one. Sometimes, I justified it with a bit of righteousness: *We won't squander money on such things.* I puffed up on the inside: *I couldn't possibly justify a diamond against the needs of the world.* Or the greatest judgment in my mind: *I never want to be one of those bejeweled women I see in designer clothes and expensive cars.* My husband was largely unaware of this drama that was going on in me.

But the reality is: I couldn't let myself get a ring because I wanted it too badly.

For years I really wanted a pretty ring. I would look at friends' rings, and I'd try them on. I would pine for them. I'd come home talking about them. I would pass by a jewelry store and linger a little too long at the windows.

I would officiate a wedding, and I'd look down at the bride's ring finger and do a quick mental calculation. I might feel a twist of envy. For more than a decade I couldn't let myself get a ring *because getting one meant too much to me.* Even while this internal drama is embarrassing to admit, it points out the place where accumulation begins to trap us. Getting a stupid ring was too important to me. And when I realized how important it was, I realized that I shouldn't—I couldn't—get it. Because it was going to take my heart. As long as I wanted something that badly, I shouldn't have it. The power of that desire was too much.

It was twenty years before I felt the freedom to put a diamond ring on. That was five years ago, and even now, sometimes I just have to take it off. Put it away for a few weeks—so it doesn't become too powerful.

Maybe you find that a silly example or perhaps you can relate perfectly. I suspect that when we examine our own areas of craving, they would tend to be just as small—like small pieces of manna we are hoarding. For some of us it's a prestigious school. For others it's our home, a car, a lifestyle, an image. It's not just an external want; it's an internal fear.

Sell it. Give it. Offer it. Take it off. Put it away. It's going to strangle you.

We all have something—some kind of "stuff" making a claim on our hearts. On our devotion. On the energy in us that was meant for love. It's taking away our freedom. It's taking away our ability to respond to Jesus. To anyone. It's sucking something precious out of us. The question is: What's the one thing you don't want to give up? That's the best place to start looking at what's holding you back.

Mark writes that the rich young man goes away sad. He had spent years getting what he had. How could he think seriously about giving it up? Who would he be without his stuff? But I think one person must have been even sadder than the man was. I have to believe Jesus' eyes filled with tears as he saw the suave young man in the elegant robes walk away.

Jesus was the only one in that encounter who realized just how much was being lost. Jesus knew that the drive for more wasn't only stealing the life the man had but also the future that might have been his as well. Too late would he realize what his life might have meant, the relationships he might have had, the work he might have done.

Give it away.

It's not easy. It's scary. You don't know what Jesus is going to ask next. You can't predict what he's going to do. Just like the Hebrews in captivity couldn't have really imagined what their new home was going to mean to them and how costly it would be to get there.

But the least we can expect when we begin to release our claim on accumulated resources is this: Our accumulated resources will begin to release their claim on us. And that outcome is worth the struggle to let go. It's all worth it to wake up confident that you already possess everything necessary for the day at hand. To go to bed assured that you lived simply and justly. Even better—to be free of the endless ache of needing more and needing to prove your worth. And to know that the path you're walking is one that leads toward home is perhaps the best outcome there is.

We can be more than the sum of our resources. We can have freedom. We can have love.

4

Hiding Behind Masks

I **immediately noticed a dissimilar beige paper** in Sumner's bundle of "parent pleasers." Our eight-year-old had come home from Sunday school with a particularly large heap this week—an untidy stack of perforated worksheets and brightly colored construction paper. It was thick paper, ragged and heavy with glue. Dried beans and corn outlined Mary and Joseph. I pulled out the single, neatly folded sheet of beige writing paper. It simply had two names on it: My husband's and mine. And next to the names, these words: "Pray this week!" It was the writing of his Sunday school teacher, and the casual cursive penmanship made me immediately suspect this was a note she had written to herself.

I froze. What had my son said? What horrible thing did he tell her that would make her remind herself to pray for us? What arguments had he reported during "sharing" time? How much detail did he go into? Those were the panicked questions of the first minute. But they were quickly followed by this weird defensiveness I felt welling up in me.

I'm sure anyone would have said the same thing! I can take care of my own concerns! I certainly don't need her worrying about me! And that final, somewhat desperate, all-too-familiar insight: *Who gave her the right to judge me anyway?*

The reality was that no one was judging anyone. Except me, judging me.

I knew this within minutes, of course. (But yes, I did confirm it with a phone call later on that night.) It turns out the teachers were thoughtfully praying for the families of their students. We were simply the next very fortunate recipients of their care—their love.

Funny how love wasn't the first thing that came to my mind. Fear had gripped me instead. I worried that we had been outed—someone was finally going to see the real family behind the nice front door.

One of the most intractable patterns I have managed to forge into my frame of mind is this fear of *being found out*. Perhaps we're all scared of being exposed. Likely every single one of us has something we are protecting, defending and disguising. Our antennae go up the instant we perceive some kind of threat to our secret selves.

From our jobs to our friends to our family, we want to be seen as pulling our own weight. Others expect us to achieve a certain amount, to produce a certain amount, to be good daughters and sons, supportive friends, and understanding partners. We accept these responsibilities—as we should, I think. Yet somewhere along the way, we wrap ourselves with a layer of deception or secrecy—protecting ourselves for those times where we don't finish with the flying colors we thought we should, or when our real life is heading for a nosedive. This may be the common way of living, but it's not freedom. The only path to freedom is along the road of honesty, no matter how painful. But to walk that road, I had to clearly see where I had settled for an imitation of truth. I had to name the ways that fear played out in my relationships through the habit of hiding behind the mask of self-deception, the mask of being good and the mask of self-imposed busyness.

Self-Deception

It's hard for us to imagine we could show people our real selves and still have anyone like us. So we pretend to be somebody else—essentially denying who we really are to put on the mask of someone more acceptable. We pretend to be the people we think others should see.

Public figures personify the pressure to uphold an outward persona that has long ago eroded from the inside. A few years ago Senator Larry Craig left the U.S. Senate in a scandal over whether he was soliciting sex in an airport bathroom stall. The irony is that before his toe-tapping got him in trouble, Senator Craig had long been one of the most outspoken advocates of a strict moral code. Politicians and preachers share this dark temptation of dishonesty. The very behavior we oppose can be the addiction we are battling. It's as though we climb onto the moral high ground on purpose—to ward off our own inner demons. *If I just say it enough, it will be true.*

Whether we are cheating at solitaire, elaborating on the big one that got away or protesting to our friends that "No really, everything's fine!" when virtually everything in our lives suggests otherwise, the human condition is awash in self-deceptions, large and small.

Telling the truth is always a tricky business. Because we can start to believe the stories we tell about ourselves. We begin to live into the scripts that we're reading from. They become the self-authenticating records of our actions. We are always in danger of believing our own hype.

The Hebrew Scripture gives us a well-known story of self-deceit in the second book of Samuel. It tells us about a man at the top of his world who had started believing the story he was telling about himself. No, even worse than that—he had begun to believe that his story was, in fact, the only story really going on (see 2 Samuel 11:1-27).

The army of the God of the Israelites had left Jerusalem to fight.

King David sent his faithful commander, Joab. The Israelites were winning. The text says they ravaged their enemies. They defeated the Ammonites; they besieged Rabbah on the battlefield. These military exploits trickled back to David who had stayed behind in Jerusalem. Everything was falling in place to back up the version of himself that David wanted people to see.

Just as the Israelites were rolling over their enemies and moving at liberty on the battlefield, the text uses similar language to describe the exploits David is about to have back home.

While his army went to battle, one leisurely afternoon, David rose from his couch, deciding to enjoy the spring weather from his rooftop garden. He strolled about, taking in the view of his kingdom. And then he saw her. She was bathing, obviously unaware that she was being watched, but he continued to look. After all, the woman was very beautiful, and since no one else was there, there was no chance someone might call his character into question. David made some inquiries and learned her name was Bathsheba. And she was married. Not only married, but married to one of his top warriors, Uriah. Tough break? A red light to stop and turn around? Nope, not for David. He discreetly sent a messenger to get her. He was the king and this was a command performance. While his army enjoyed their conquests, David enjoyed a conquest of his own. He had sex with her and then returned her to her home.

A month or so later, Bathsheba sends a terse two-word statement: "I'm pregnant."

Hum. That wasn't what the king expected from their single rendezvous.

I'm pregnant. With those words, David must work fast. In quick order, he sends word to his commander, Joab, on the field, "Bring me Uriah." David makes several attempts to get Uriah to return to his wife. It's a show to legitimize the pregnancy. But Uriah refuses to go back home. He's a faithful warrior. "How could I?" Uriah protests.

"How could I go home when the ark of God is on the battlefield?"

Okay. So that plan didn't work. But now the clock is really ticking for David, and if he doesn't take care of this little problem soon, his whole image could crumble. So David sends a letter to the front lines to Joab (a letter carried by Uriah, if you can imagine that) telling Joab to make sure Uriah is in the heaviest fighting, then pull back the troops so that (I'm quoting here) "he may be struck down and die."

Joab complies. Uriah is killed. The widow Bathsheba mourns for her dead husband, and then the king sends for her, and she becomes his fourth wife.

End of story.

At least, it could have been the end. Hey, if this was only David's story to tell that might have been the end of it. His cover-up might have held. He could have congratulated himself on being a good guy, kindly taking in a widow without means.

Kind of like the rich young ruler, we could have read the story and just felt sad that David wasn't the king that he might have been. Another life not lived to the full potential.

But David's story, it turns out, wasn't the only story going on here. The prophet Samuel keeps unwinding a bigger story. Because "The thing David had done displeased the Lord."

See, if this were only David's story to write, there wouldn't have been any problem. If our stories are ours alone, then we don't need to wrestle with conflict between our ideals and our actions. If your story is yours alone, then go ahead—believe your own hype. Immerse yourself in your PR spin. Keep on making those rationalizations. It's your own story, your own desires, your own ambitions—and don't let anyone else tell you otherwise! That's what our culture tells us, doesn't it?

David could have continued his secret life—and so could we. But it comes with the cost of loneliness.

And it can happen without notice can't it? Joseph Ellis is a Pulitzer Prize–winning historian and a popular professor at Mount Holyoke College.[1] Decades ago, he entered into a sort of exercise in imagination with his students, teaching them about what it might have meant to fight in Vietnam. In the retelling, year after year, Ellis began to share more about his own experience, described what it felt like to parachute into the jungle with the 101st Airborne, revealed the inner workings of service on General Westmoreland's staff. He divulged some details in interviews with the media as his books gained honors and attention. His service in Vietnam became part of his official biography. The sticking point was: These things never happened!

It was fabricated. But after decades of repeating it, Ellis began living that story as if it were true. In an editorial on his suspension from Mount Holyoke, the *New York Times* speculated on his motives:

> Why should a man as successful as Mr. Ellis, whose books are those rare creatures, best-selling works of history, feel compelled to reinvent his past? One might almost suppose that he was not so much reinventing his past as confirming his present, projecting his current degree of success backward in time, living up to a version of himself.[2]

Self-deception lurks in denials, double-mindedness, rationalizations, cover-ups and cover stories, excuses, attributions of blame, and evasions of responsibility.

Daniel Goleman, the Harvard researcher who wrote *Vital Lies, Simple Truths: The Psychology of Self-Deception*, said often we engage in self-deception to defend against a perceived threat to our self-image.[3] We want to be those generous people (so we make one contribution to prove it to ourselves). We want to be honest (so no, we don't cheat on our taxes). We want to be in control (so no, we have no drinking problem).

Being Good

For some of us the most elaborate mask we wear is the one that is the most socially approved mask—at least in religious circles. It's the mask of being good. Now this is something I happen to know quite a lot about. I'd say it's disturbing just how familiar I am with the mask of being good.

A few years ago my husband and I spent a week in Italy. Some people go to soak up the atmosphere, indulge in the food and wine and—well, other desires. But us? We went to church after museum to church after museum . . . you get the idea. Centuries ago, builders constructed each church as an act of devotion and worship. Many artists produced paintings and sculpture with similarly ardent intentions.

Now I have a bent toward pious acts. I know this about myself. I have a streak in me that is wired toward religious bean counting. I'm drawn to practices like praying a particular prayer X times a day, doing a succession of detailed practices and the like. Similarly, I am prone to legends and unexplainable mystery. Naturally, in Rome, bathed in the pungent aroma of incense, surrounded by the ever-vigilant stone saints and attentive to the actions of the pious pilgrims, my inner Catholic was really getting a workout.

After visiting the Church of San Giovanni, a famous stop, I noticed the guidebook's reference to the nearby church of the Scala Sancta. The description had me hooked. The church was supposedly built around the very steps of Pilate's palace in Jerusalem. These forty or so steps *were the very ones Christ descended after being sentenced to death by Pilate! They had been brought from Jerusalem by Helen, Constantine's mother!*

"Listen to this, Terry!" I exclaimed to my husband. The guidebook went on to say that ascending these steps on your knees had been a longstanding act of devotion since the year 1000 or so. In fact, these were the very stairs Martin Luther had been ascending when he suddenly understood the meaning of a verse from the book of Romans that "The just shall live by faith" (Romans 1:17 KJV). Halfway up the stairs, as the truth of this freedom sank in, Luther immediately stood and walked the rest of the way, shoulders back and head high.

My rationalist husband scoffed at this. "Don't tell me you really believe that three hundred years later Constantine's mother is in Jerusalem and happens to find these stairs that happen to still be standing? You don't really believe they quarried marble and carted it down from Jerusalem for these kinds of relatively unimportant buildings." Blah. Blah. Blah.

None of his words made any difference to me. I was determined to ascend those stairs on my knees. Determined to have my own religious epiphany. So, while Terry calmly walked up the nonsacred stairs—the stairs for the religious wannabes—I knelt on that first cold marble step.

Immediately I knew I'd made a mistake. A really bad mistake. The searing pain that radiated from my left knee still causes me to wince as I think about it. But what could I do about it then? I was surrounded by other pilgrims—mostly elderly ladies dressed in black. Tenderly I swung my right hip forward jerking my knee to the next step.

The second step. Only thirty-eight to go.

Painfully, so painfully I picked my way up those steps. Sometimes I would put my hands down on the stone as if in an act of prayer, but really, I was supporting my weight to offer some relief to my knees. At step fifteen or twenty I had my religious experience all right: It was a vision of me getting into a squat and rushing up a few additional steps while my octogenarian friends were bowed in prayer. That kept me going for a bit.

This is a picture of the mask of being good: me, on my knees, longing to deceive and desperately wishing it was all over.

I had fallen into that trap that pious actions would make me more holy, more lovable. More . . . *special* to God.

I can so easily lose sight of the reality that I am a child of God, gifted by God, hard-wired by God for greatness. That's not a challenge to live up to but a promise to live into. And that changes everything for me. And you too. It means we don't have to prove our specialness or our goodness or our worthiness. We are free to simply live into God's promise.

Benjamin Zander, the conductor of the Boston Philharmonic and a professor at the New England Conservatory of Music, has a wonderful example of this in his book *The Art of Possibility*.[4]

As you can imagine, to really *play* music is to do more than just master the notes. The notes are just the mechanics. Any parent or sibling who has suffered through those early lessons can attest to that. Great musicians are marked by what they do with the music—how their pain, their hope, their love are bound up and given voice through their unique interpretation of the score at hand.

The great works of music call upon qualities of nobility and warmth and sensitivity—love! But then we have this music education system stuck in a vortex of competition, backbiting, subservience and status seeking. How can a system like that produce players that are free enough to access these deeper places?

Zander decided that in his classes he would begin by giving all the students an A. That's it. Everybody gets an A. In fact, he has them write an essay during the first week expressing what they will be like at the end of the term of having been A students. For the rest of the term, instead of the A being the standard against which the students are judged and Zander enforces, the A becomes the reality that they can accept, freeing both teacher and student to accomplish something great.

God doesn't ask us to be perfect. God says we are good enough. Simply live in that promise and in that tension.

It's common to deceive ourselves and to put on the mask of being good. But there's another mask, and this one is a sort of equal opportunity mask; people of all stripes wear it, and it's pretty irresistible because we're always praised for it. It's called being really, really busy.

Being Busy

It was snowing, with temperatures in the single digits and nearing darkness by the time I arrived at the house, high in the mountains of Colorado. Carrying a few bags of groceries, some sweat clothes, my Bible and prayer journal, I settled in to begin my ten-day silent retreat.

I had done a few shorter retreats, but this was my first attempt at something beyond a weekend. *Ah! A week and a half to pray, think, meditate! In silence!*

And that was the problem. Because it was silent and it was just me, after the first day, I was bored out of my mind.

I arrived Sunday night. I woke up Monday morning with high expectations. Got myself all situated. Prayed for the church, prayed a good portion of the way through the church directory, prayed for all the needs I could think of. Feeling very satisfied, I looked up at the clock and it was 9:15. I had been at it for a total of forty-five minutes, and there was *nothing* left to pray for!

That was a scary moment. The magnitude of what it meant to be silent for that long struck me like a semi-truck. I started to panic. It was *too quiet*. Nine and a half days left.

There was a time when I seemed to regularly land in these situations. Set a high bar, plan, struggle, achieve—and panic. A few years ago Shane Claiborne visited our church. Shane is one of the pioneers behind the Simple Way community in Philadelphia.[5] It's a kind of groovy, shared-living arrangement where folks have intentionally pared down their lives and lifestyles in order to just "be" with their neighbors.

Two days after spending the weekend with Shane, my mind was still racing from the great stories he had told. I was filled with all these glorious thoughts and ideas for myself and for my family. *Communal living!* Well, you know, I have thought before about obtaining a large old warehouse and moving in with a group of like-minded people, sharing communal meals and having this great garden in the back. In my fantasy things were more orderly than the relaxed spirit of the Simple Way, but God could free me from that, I was sure.

I was enamored with visions of doing some of the cool things Shane's community does. Like, they sew their own clothes. *Well, hey,* I thought, *I can sew!* I won the 4-H award for my cross-stitched apron one year! I can start sewing again for the family! That's a way of getting back to basics!

The list went on. I remembered Shane saying in our Q&A on Sunday afternoon about how the Simple Way people redirected their plumbing pipes to repurpose the water from the kitchen sink in order to operate their toilets. "It just makes sense!" he said. "What right do we have to waste drinking water when one billion people in the world don't have access to clean water?" Even though I wasn't sure how reusing my sink water would actually help someone else have clean water, it seemed like a solidarity thing so I grabbed my *Fix It Fast, Fix It Right* home repair book to see if they covered basic plumbing principles.

While I was considering these simple living options, I happened to be cooking. I was leaving town for a conference the following week, so I was trying to get a lot of meals made and frozen. There was a lot of chopping, dicing and cutting to do.

I have a food processor; I have a nut chopper. But that didn't seem very *simple*. I mean, knowing that there are people out there re-routing their water supply for their toilets, I felt guilty wasting electricity on kitchen gadgets.

Sometime in the mid-afternoon, while I was laboriously chopping two cups of pecans with a meat mallet, it struck me that maybe this isn't what faithful living is all about. That the kingdom of God I am so smitten with—the presence of God renewing, recreating, the idea that our lives can reflect the life of Christ—isn't about careening one from message to another, and it isn't simply transferring the call some have received and pasting it on to my particular life.

Action isn't the place where an authentic life starts. Actions are purposeless unless they reflect something deeper, unless they mirror our heart's posture. They reflect a disposition—a certain centeredness out of which our accomplishments flow. Ultimately, what saints (Shane included) are offering cannot be truncated into specific actions. It's not about communal living or helping people or using less electricity. For Shane and the people at the Simple Way, these actions are just the blossoming result of a rooted life. They are living a story larger than their own. When we're isolated behind our masks, bound to our own story as though that's all there is, our actions, however well-intended, amount to just another anxious presence in an anxious world. That is not the outcome I had hoped for when I spent an extra hour chopping away in the kitchen. I was longing for the sense of oneness, the sense of unity I experienced midway through that ten-day retreat, when I was finally forced to let go of my need to *do* something with my prayers and silence.

I wanted *shalom* life. *Shalom* is a Hebrew word with many shades of meaning: well-being, settled, complete, peaceful. *Shalom* is wholeness. *Shalom* is a noun, an adjective, an adverb. Grammatically speaking, it's a big tent. It's a word meant to convey a very large experience. It's the peace of mind and sense of freedom that come from knowing you're going to be okay.

That's what I was after. I wanted this freedom to live. I wanted this almost carefree attitude to time and obligation, coupled with the presence of love and power. Jesus lived the presence of shalom. His disciples felt it. Wherever Jesus was, shalom directed the activity. It's an active sabbath way of life.

Much of our religious experience would tell us that the way to make Jesus present in the world is simply to do more. Isn't that how it works? Work harder!

Lawyers get paid by the hour. So do babysitters, as my daughter reminded me. Factory workers often get paid by the piece. Real estate agents get paid when the house gets sold. It's an economic rule of production. We make the surplus happen. So if you want to bring forth the kingdom of God, well, you've got to get out there and do it, right?

I had forgotten the kingdom of God is an upside-down place.

This mask of being busy is what the ancient church fathers understood when they talked about the sin of sloth. In contemporary language we've made *sloth* into a synonym for laziness. But that wasn't what it was for the desert fathers, Pope Gregory, Thomas Aquinas or Dante. At its heart the sin of sloth was a kind of disordered attachment. A kind of malaise that can disguise itself in any number of ways—including frantic sixty-hour workweeks, endless emails and calendar scheduling.[6]

You could be very, very busy and have your soul in the clenches of sloth because sloth isn't inactivity but *purposeless* activity. Sloth is caring too much about the wrong things or not making enough space for the right ones.

In my life sloth can keep me very engaged—just not in the things that are really important. It's my classic distraction. *I must first organize my desk, put in a load of laundry and prep dinner before I can even think of writing against that deadline.*

The Gospel of Luke introduces us to a couple of hit-it-early-hit-it-hard guys getting their first glimpse of shalom, the real kingdom of God (see Luke 5:1-11).

These fishermen were worn out from their work. They went out on their boat at dusk the night before, and now it was the next morning. They were weary from exertion and discouraged at their lack of results. They didn't have much to show for their efforts. In fact, they returned with empty nets. Nothing. Working all night, and nothing.

That has to be one of the worst feelings in the world—when you are busting it and you have pretty much nothing to show for it. You

have been working and working. Maybe at your job, maybe at a relationship, maybe trying to make the world safer, healthier, more just.
Or like me in the kitchen or on retreat—knocking yourself out to
live a simple life, a silent life.

The men don't seem to even notice the commotion stirring just
down the beach. A crowd is pressing around Jesus so closely that
they've backed him up to the lake. Jesus is so squeezed that he is
seeking some way to get some space between himself and these
people clamoring for his attention.

But the fishermen don't notice. They're busy, scrubbing away at
their nets, doing their job. It's Jesus who notices them. He comes to
them and asks them to take him out in their boat.

According to Luke's story there's no indication that they really
know or care who Jesus is. The text only says that Jesus taught the
crowd. Jesus just seems to be doing his thing, and the fishermen are
working in their boat, doing their thing, bone-tired, wondering why
they didn't catch anything. Being decent guys, they help out Jesus by
giving him a place on their boat to get a little space from the crowd.

It's after Jesus has finished teaching the people that he turns
toward Simon and says, "Put out into deeper water and let down
your nets for a catch."

*Oh, come on! We've been doing that all night! And we have nothing
to show for it!*

It strikes me as a good illustration of what happens in our lives
when we are doing our thing and Jesus is doing his thing, and the only
connection is that we happen to be sitting in the same boat. Sloth.

The remedy for sloth isn't work, it's love. It really is that simple.
Love is resting on you right now. Pressing down on you. Sitting next
to you. This is the remedy for sloth, for the purposeless activity we
chase as we wear the mask of being busy: to be reminded again that
we live in a world suffused with grace, brimming with hope and
overflowing with God's life. With *shalom.*

Sloth turns away from the demands of love. When love demands engagement, sloth declines to get involved. When love asks us to be alert, sloth whispers, *It's okay, you're tired.* When love demands fidelity, sloth would sneak in lesser affections.

When love declares that our days are important and our lives have eternal significance, sloth sighs and says, *We rise to just do the same things we did the day before.* And when love says that the world is crying out for healing, sloth puts up her hands and shrugs her shoulders with a bored *Whatever.*

Where sloth might say, *You are a failure—you rise only to fall again,* God answers, *Shalom.* God answers, *There is no one so lost that my eternal love cannot find you.*

Self-deception, being good, being busy—those are the common ways we can hide from honesty. And when we hide from honesty, we hide from the source of love and from the agents of love in our lives. I learned if I was going to establish a new life in God and with others, I had to do the difficult work of being honest. I had to take off my masks. All of them.

5

Behind the Mask

After a fairly insular junior high experience in our rural area of Florida, I went to a high school that was in the process of being re-districted. There were a slew of new people in school, and this high school was about triple the size of my junior high school. These new kids included a lot of "city" kids. Kids whose dads didn't burn their trash behind their house. Kids who didn't have well water. Kids who didn't have party-line telephones. (Yes, party-line telephones. Seems like eternity ago now.)

Naturally, the kids from town all looked a lot better, they dressed better, their schools had been better. Or so it all seemed in my fourteen-year-old mind. These girls became the cheerleaders, the class representatives, the club officers. I felt like I was on the outside looking in—until it came time for the fall talent show and the spring Kiwanis Club variety show. Then all these cute, perky cheerleaders came looking for me. Suddenly I went from being a nobody to one of the most sought-after kids in school. Because all these pop star wannabes needed a pianist, and I was the best pianist we had. That's not saying a lot now, but back then it said plenty.

I did whatever it took to rehearse with these girls. Trying to be like them. Trying to make them like me. Transposing the keys, reworking music sections that were out of their range, even standing in line for them at registration. For two years I thought that because they liked what I could do for them, they would like me as well. And for two years it ended up the same way: I would get a party invitation the week before the show. But the week after? They would pass me in the hallway without even a nod.

I was used. But over time I also began to recognize that I was a user as well. I was willing to use my gift to try to manipulate my peers—those peers with names like Heather and Buffy—into liking me.

There was no particular reason why they should like me. We had nothing in common. In fact, I didn't really like them especially. But I liked what I thought I could get from them. Status. Popularity. Importance.

There's nothing like taking off a mask to make you realize why you were wearing one in the first place. The truth of my high school experience—perhaps yours as well—was that I was deeply afraid of being unnoticed. Insignificant. Taking off the mask reveals a fear that's been with us so long that we hardly notice it anymore. For me the fear functions as a ubiquitous backdrop—kind of like the beat of trance music—pulsing below the surface.

It manifests itself in the sneaking feeling that if I don't make my presence felt, then no one else will even know I'm here. It's the feeling that it all comes down to me, and if I don't convey how important I am, then it's likely no one else will find out on their own. And then I'll be left with—nothing.

I know that sounds small. But the reality is that I'm not alone. Far from it. Many of us believe we have to think of ourselves all the time because deep down we fear no one else is thinking of us.

Does it seem too obvious to point that this perspective sounds a lot like the world of being a teenager? The manic self-absorption of our teen years can leave many of us with scripts that continue to replay themselves over our lives. I watch my kids try on different habits, friends and personas as they locate their real identity. And I wince because I know just how many moments of high school will imprint themselves on their memories, continuing to work fear into their lives long after the moment has passed.

It took me a while to see that it was fear behind my desire to be indispensible to others. *Without me*, I've rationalized, *you wouldn't be able to be the "you" you want to be.* Whacked? Absolutely.

Removing the Mask—to Think of Ourselves Less

Beneath your mask, fear may tell you that you might be empty. When I used other people, it was all about my needing to strengthen my ego from some source outside myself. Needing others to tell me I was worth it. Because underneath that mask I believed I wasn't.

Jesus applied the same principle Benjamin Zander was going to use in his music class thousands of years later: Everyone starts with an A, or in the language of Jesus, everyone begins blessed. And because everyone begins blessed, we don't have to think so much about how to make sure we get the blessings coming to us. Instead we can trust the blessing, take some risks and live in the freedom of God's certainty. Jesus was so confident in this that he advised his followers to "deny themselves and take up their cross and follow me" (Matthew 16:24).

How on earth could self-denial be the antidote to our fear of not being valued?

It's helpful to see that Jesus says this to his close friend and perhaps most well-known disciple, Peter. Jesus and the crew had left the lush countryside of Caesarea Philippi and were making their way south to Jerusalem. Jesus was trying to explain how death is a necessary condition for life, when Peter, in a pique of self-help motivational therapy, suggested that suffering wasn't all that necessary.

Most often we read those words and they conjure up images of depravation, of battling temptation, of doing war with the flesh. Through history, that's what the church has often taught with these words. Our view of self-denial has been kind of screwed up. In the way these words were interpreted in the Middle Ages, the call to "deny yourself" led to an almost crazed fixation on the self. It led to self-flagellation and asceticism. Like the evil albino monk in Dan Brown's *The Da Vinci Code* whipping himself in remorse and self-loathing.

That might be an extreme example, but the church has regularly given the message that self-denial is a way of "teaching yourself a lesson." It's sin control at the basest level. But self-denial for the sake of sin control is just another expression of our own longing for control. It doesn't have anything to do with what Jesus was getting at. Just giving up things doesn't make you a Christian; it just makes you empty.

Self-denial, or denying yourself, is an idiom that means "love less." Jesus was asking Peter to give a lower priority to his own concerns and to turn his attention away from himself. To focus instead on Jesus.

It's not about thinking less of ourselves, it's thinking of ourselves less. When we are able to spend less time thinking about ourselves, we free up space in our minds to focus on those around us. The relationships that matter, the causes that matter, the values that matter.

Our fear that we have to think about ourselves all the time because we doubt anyone else is thinking about us is, ironically, what separates us from the very ones who could assist us.

One of the earliest Hebrew stories ever told concerned the sudden insight about this very concept given to a totally unexceptional man named Abraham (see Genesis 12).

This is the state of Abraham's world: The human family is in ruins. Brother killing brother. Humanity is dislocated from their land and from each other when God's voice comes to this man who is not known for anything remarkable or even particularly distinctive. It's never clear in this story why God comes to Abraham and not his brothers Nahor or Haran.

But this lone Mesopotamian is singled out. And without apology, without explanation, without any indication of the man's particular worthiness or competence or anything else, God promises Abraham that he is going to be great. That he will be the father of a great nation and that through him, "all the families of the earth shall bless themselves by you."

In fact, the way the Hebrew Scriptures document this story, it almost appears as if God is reversing the curses that were rendered to Adam and Eve in the garden creation story. In place of exile, God is supplying a new home. The pain of losing a son is offset by the blessing of children too numerous to be counted. And the uncooperative soil, the fruit of which could only be wrought by the sweat of Adam's brow, God is promising to replace with abundance.

And all of this is supposed to happen through one man's newfound relationship with his Creator and with others. I remember reading a little devotional one time that in a very simple way stated a very obvious point: If you want to be full of God, then you'll need to be less full of yourself. This is what Abraham did—he thought less about himself than he did about God.

Removing the Mask—to Find Freedom

You see, beneath your mask, fear may tell you that you can't afford to be generous. Maintaining a posture of kindness and generosity in the face of fear is really hard—generosity is concrete evidence that we are living just a little bit freer. This kind of generosity is what we see throughout Abraham's life, particularly in his relationship with his nephew Lot.

One of the first times we see Lot and his uncle Abraham is in the thirteenth chapter of the book of Genesis as they are returning from a sojourn in Egypt. The trip has made them both wildly rich. They have so much stuff that the land simply can't sustain their combined cattle, sheep and people. The time has come for them to separate their households. Abraham takes Lot to a high mountain where they can look out over an expansive valley. From this vantage point, they can choose the property where each will settle.

The old man, Abraham, should have been the one to choose first, but he is free enough to allow his ambitious nephew the opportunity to decide first. Abraham doesn't need any more stuff. He's not pining for more. Abraham is free from the allure of acquisition. As opposed to the rich man we met earlier, Abraham has a sort of holy indifference to the accumulation of more.

But on the mountain that day, Abraham stands alongside his nephew, Lot, all twitching and young. Lot is well-established, but he's hungry for something more. And his desire to define himself with the best—the most—leaves no room for generosity. Lot ignores custom, respect or deference for his elder and selects the choicest parcel of land. As the text describes it, "Lot looked around and saw that the whole plain of the Jordan . . . was well watered, like the garden of the LORD, like the land of Egypt. . . . So Lot chose for himself the whole plain" (Genesis 13:10-11 NIV).

For Lot, it didn't matter that the plain of Jordan was known for its sinful behaviors. It didn't matter that his uncle should have chosen first. It didn't matter that he already had plenty. Lot had an itch he had to scratch, a hunger he had to fill. He thought that the way to go about filling it was to *take care of myself first,* which is the way many of us choose as well.

If we follow his story, in a few years, we will find Lot running for his life with simply the clothes on his back and the company of his two daughters. His insatiable self-absorption will lead to the destruction of everything he cherished: his wife, his wealth, his reputation will all be destroyed. In choosing the choicest place to live,

Lot also chose to live near cities known for their riotous behavior. It's not long before the young, ambitious Lot has become one of the city fathers in a city known for its callousness toward the weak and poor.

Lot barely escapes the destruction of Sodom—vacating this city only when impending doom is unavoidable. And by the time he does leave, it's evident Lot has lost any semblance of a moral compass. He's sacrificed everything on the altar of narcissism. But again, Lot didn't start out this way! Abraham had treated this young man as a son. Lot knew something of Abraham's God, witnessed something of Abraham's freedom, saw something of Abraham's faith. But his fears planted in him a "me first" attitude—an attitude that he watered and cultivated through the years. The years of grasping, of gripping, of taking—it all slowly anesthetized him to the reality of who he was becoming.

Anita has been my friend for years. She and I have worked the same block parties and have enjoyed the same book group. We have also aged together. Or I should say, we should have aged together. Anita is spending close to a small fortune—a fortune she doesn't have—to pay for Botox and fills, for increasingly expensive spa treatments and increasingly frequent appointments with personal trainers. When I once asked her what this is all about, her answer was so simple: "What are you talking about? This is what every woman I know is doing."

Explaining that not *every woman* she knows is doing this seemed liked splitting hairs. The point is, many women do just what Anita is doing. It started gradually and has become a way of trying to keep the fear of really looking our age at bay. We are spending and worrying and exercising our way into the very same place Lot did.

Lot's story didn't have to end this way. And we don't have to live with our fears feeding a false sense of need, with our debt ever climbing, our hearts pounding harder and our feet running faster and faster to just to stay ahead.

We have not reached the end. *It is not too late for us.* We were born to live as free as Abraham, the one who stood on that hill and calmly said, "Which one would you like? You choose first."

The Perfect Stranger

Beneath your mask, fear may tell you that you must be perfect. Our masks indeed hold our fear of being empty and our fear that we must be everything if we are to be anything. But they also contain one other reality that many of us are loath to reveal: *our complete and ordinary humanity.*

The most prolific writer in the New Testament had an image problem. No matter how much this missionary talked about love, suffered for love, acted in love, people had a hard time believing he was for real. Sure, we know him now as Saint Paul. But at the time of his writing, he was plain Paul, the missionary who had to support himself by making tents on the side. Paul's credibility suffered. He didn't promote himself the way people thought he should.

In his second letter to the church in the Greek city of Corinth, Paul defends himself against some personal attacks. There are some among these Corinthians who see themselves as superapostles. It sounds like they are having wild success in their preaching. They look impressive. They act impressive. Against these dazzlers Paul somehow doesn't seem to measure up (see 2 Corinthians 11).

The people in Corinth have already complained that Paul doesn't show off his success in the manner they would like. They have called his speech "contemptible," and Paul concedes himself that his speech is, well, unskilled.

And then there is this mysterious issue with what many scholars believe is a physical deformity that Paul himself was once desperate to get rid of. This "thorn in my flesh," as Paul calls it. For whatever reason, God simply doesn't seem to see fit to rid Paul of it.

I can hear the taunts that may have been leveled at him: a faith healer who can't heal himself. Paul seems so ordinary. Who would want to follow someone like that?

Who among us hasn't wanted at some time to be a part of a group that looks a certain way and acts a certain way? Some little community that seems put together, that really feels like it has its act together. I often come across reports from experts on church growth saying that people choose churches by walking in, looking around and asking themselves, *Do these people look like who I want to look like?* We want to be around people who can offer us an idealized vision of ourselves.

Paul's on the defensive. But not just for himself. Something larger is at stake. It's more than just a criticism leveled at an individual. Paul is worried that these superapostles may undermine the very message God has for the world—the very message Paul has committed his life to. He's trying to get the message across that super signs, persuasive speech, powerful demonstrations—this idealized community—are not the answer.

Paul is desperate for them to see that in their groping attempts to appear to be better than someone else, in their empty boasting about who they are, in their inflated sense of self, they are in danger of reducing the very message they say they believe. They are in danger of never having the true power of God revealed in their community.

The Corinthian community was looking for God in the extraordinary. Looking for God in the way of demonstrable power and dazzling light shows. They were looking for a God who made them look good. I know this temptation. This is one of the biggest ways I keep fear at bay: by looking beautifully invincible. But here's the thing. The very ways I bury my fear also bury something else: authenticity, realness, honesty. And ultimately these actions do just what self-absorption did for Lot; they will keep me from the very life I want the most.

My friend Suzanne is a professor at one of the most prestigious institutions in Chicago. She is smart, successful and confident. She is also a bundle of fear right underneath the surface. She can't *afford* to say, "I don't know." She can't risk uncertainty. She can't risk not looking like she has it all together. If she does, her image will suffer.

Paul looks at this mentality and says *no way*. God will never be found making people look good. Don't be impressed by those who have glib answers. Don't equate God's power with human impressiveness. No way.

You see, if God doesn't use ordinary people—"jars of clay," in Paul's words—then there's no hope for guys like Paul (see 2 Corinthians 4). If God doesn't work through people who are weak-kneed and self-conscious, then there's no hope. If God doesn't use people who have committed grievous offenses and done horrific things, people who have lied and cheated and stolen and even committed murder, then there's no hope for Paul. There's no hope for those people in Corinth. And there's no hope for us.

So here he is. Saint Paul. One of the most compelling figures in any movement anywhere, practically begging them to understand: *I am nothing more than a clay pot. I am something so exceedingly average, so yawningly common that I have nothing to boast about. I have nothing to brag about.*

If I must boast, then I will tell you about my humiliations and weaknesses: I will tell you about the time I was smuggled out of a building, helplessly lowered down the wall in a basket, in fear for my life. I will tell you about the time I was shipwrecked, my clothes torn and ratty, while I rooted around for food. I will tell you about the time I was run out of town. I will tell you about the things that should shame me the most.

Let me tell you, he says, *about all the things that prove my ordinariness, my common frailty with you. Let me tell you about all the ways I have failed, where my courage failed me, when I was misunderstood and failed to use the right words, when I didn't make the best decisions. Let me tell you of my weakness. Because that's where I see most clearly the power of God in my life.*

Let me tell you that I am just a clay pot, an earthen vessel, and then let me even show you all of the cracks in this vessel.

The chorus of a Leonard Cohen's "Anthem" says:

Ring the bells that still can ring
Forget your perfect offering
There is a crack—a crack in everything
That's how the light gets in.[1]

Oh, it's hard to believe that, isn't it? We drink the milk of a culture that believes we must all be "above average." Our weaknesses are the things we beat ourselves up for. We turn our mistakes over and over and over again in our minds, wishing we could have a do over.

We don't want to be clay pots in the first place. We want to be crystal or porcelain or polished marble. But even if we have to acknowledge that we're clay, we certainly don't want to show each other the places that are chipped and nicked. The broken places, the cracked places. The places that have mold from too much moisture and have become bleached from too much wear.

We ruminate on those embarrassments, those things we're ashamed of and long to hide, and we tell ourselves to get it together. We try to conceal those cracks—we're eager to start making repairs. But our repair work is never quite done. We can't seem to hear Paul pleading with us to go ahead and leave it undone.

I began preaching as a pastor in September 2000. And I was nervous. So nervous that for the first several months I kept a bar stool behind the pulpit in case I got lightheaded.

The first year or so, I had these vivid flashbacks to when I was a ninth grader at my big, new high school. I was very, very thin, and like many of us I was very self-conscious. I had to deliver a message to a class of eleventh and twelfth graders. And it looked like the entire cheerleading squad and half of the football team was in that room. I was neither. As I started to give the message, I got so nervous that tears started to form in my eyes. Which was, of course, immediately noticed.

I heard whispers moving along the room as I stood there feeling increasingly self-conscious and wishing I could just melt away. This is the scene I relived for a long time.

I know that when I have told a few people about how nervous I get (less now than at the beginning), I get these smiles of disbelief. Like I'm pulling their leg or something. In those moments I feel like I can understand a little bit of how Paul felt when he tried to help the people at Corinth see what they were missing. And I want to pull their face back to me and say, "No! You don't understand! Standing up and sharing the Word of God is something that God is doing in me!" I take a very reluctant, very weak step forward and then God comes swooping down and says, *Okay. I'll take over from here.*

I suspect God wants to do this in every area of our lives. My experience with taking this little leap of faith has made me wonder if God doesn't want to offer this same freedom in all of our areas of weakness and brokenness. Imagine! Living like you have nothing to hide! Imagine living without the driver of fear.

Maybe God's saying, *Go ahead. It's safe to put down that mask and let people know you're undone. You don't have to be perfect. You don't even have to be above average.* If you've been burned from your past encounters, hesitant to go forward, the truth is, God is a lot more gentle with us than we are with ourselves and with each other. God puts a lot more affirmation and trust in us and the "unadorned clay pots of our ordinary lives" than we ever do.

I often marvel that Jesus never felt a compelling need to write down his life's teaching. He assembled this *deeply flawed* little band of outsiders and left it to them to document his life and continue his work. He never saw the need to keep a journal around, just in case that rag-tag group around him got it wrong.

Think about that. Imagine how much trust and confidence Jesus placed in a group of people who failed again and again.

He was content to use Peter in his impulsiveness and Matthew in his unsavory relationship with a corrupt government and John and James in their petty sibling rivalry. He was content to use Thomas in his doubts and Mary of Magdala with her past. Jesus was willing to stake his ministry on folks like the perfectionist Martha and the grieving Mary. Willing to let lepers and outcasts speak his message.

He didn't use these people for their strengths, he used them simply because they were willing to share their experiences of him. Their experiences of grace. The fact that they would share their experiences clumsily, weakly, inadequately didn't cause Jesus to regroup and rethink the entire enterprise. No.

At some point, people started giving each other the idea that this brokenness that once led people to fall at Jesus' feet was not good enough for Jesus or for each other. We began to see those cracks—those cracks that we all have—as mistakes we will someday be rid of. And when we aren't rid of them, we start to hide them, to squirrel them away so that others won't know that about us.

The truth is: We will die in just the same way we lived. As clay pots. Earthen vessels. And our brokenness? Instead of becoming something to hide, Jesus simply tells us it's another place in which he can love us.

Read how Julian of Norwich, a Christian mystic and nun from the fourteenth century, understood God's words to her:

> You must learn to understand that all your deficiencies, even those that come from your past sins and vicious habits, are part of my loving providence for you, and that it is just with those deficiencies, just the way you are now, that I would love you.
>
> Therefore you must overcome the habit of judging how you would make yourself acceptable to me. When you do this you

are putting your providence, your wisdom before mine. It is my wisdom that tells you, "The way you are acceptable to me, the way I want to love you, is the way you are now, with all your defects and deficiencies. I could wipe them out in a moment if I wanted to, but then I could not love you the way I want to love you, the way you are — now."[2]

"The way you are acceptable . . . is the way you are now." This is what God wants to tell you. Do you ever feel like you're used up? Like you've failed one too many times? Guess what? You're a clay vessel. You will be cracked again.

Maybe you feel drawn to a new opportunity? You want to make a difference, but you don't know what you have to give? You have something. And that something is enough. You have your weakness, your limitations, your cracks in that clay pot. You have cracks in your mask, and that's how the light gets in — through the cracks.

But what if you simply let yourself be undone, took off the mask completely and allowed the full intensity of God's light to shine unobstructed and unencumbered? What might that look like?

6

Transforming Fear

*I*f we are going to become those people we've been pretending to be—strong, courageous, honest—if we're going to become people who aren't letting fear dictate how we live our lives, we're going to need an infusion of hope, a hope big enough to quell our fears. And for that we're going to need some outside help. Left to our own devices we will keep running our tired tactics and speaking our weary words. We've learned how to protect ourselves and how to avoid the kind of people, situations and stories that might cause us to confront our status quo.

But it is possible to imagine something different. After a decade with no communication between him and his father, Will heard a testimony in church about just following the next step no matter where it may take you. He picked up the phone that Sunday afternoon to tell his father he was sorry for those years of estrangement. He didn't know how his father would react, whether his father would take any responsibility or where that phone call would take him. Will only knew he had to take the first step out of his fear of "what if?"

After several years of hearing from her cocaine-using husband

that "it will never happened again," Maria finally un̲
she had to get herself and her daughter out of his home.
me that evening from her sister's house not knowing where th̲   ̲ad
would lead, but knowing that she had to act in spite of her fears. And
by taking that step, she was making public what had once been
secret—she was exiting the cycle.

In every story I know about people who are afraid and who take a
step anyway, it seems there is a common thread—some progressive
steps—that help them break loose from the past. It begins by recognizing that help may come from unlikely, even *unknown*, places.
One of those stories that I find oddly inspiring took place in the
Gerasenes region in the Middle East (see Mark 5:1-20). Today we
know this area as the Golan Heights, the disputed land between
Israel and Syria.

The story is recorded in the Gospel written by Mark, a friend and
follower of Jesus. Matthew repeated it in his own Gospel account
with a few variations.

Gerasenes was a region of ten small towns where generally "undesirables" were housed. When Alexander the Great reigned, almost
three hundred years earlier, these cities were proud Greek outposts.

It was here that a nameless man resided. We only know him by his
condition: the demoniac. According to Mark he lived among the
tombs. Perhaps Mark makes a point of telling us this because this
man could no longer tell the difference between life and death? The
demoniac was once shackled to the rocks but now lived there without
restraints. Not physical restraints. But he was imprisoned. Isolated
and alone.

Why am I inspired by such a desperate sounding story? Because
for many of us the fears we conceal leave us in a space that's not all
that dissimilar to the man who lives among the Gerasenes. Some of
us have entered a disputed territory where we feel increasingly isolated, unknown even to ourselves.

The solutions we thought were working are working no longer, the jobs we thought we were going to retire from have evaporated, the money we thought we were going to live on has vanished, the person we thought we were going to live with has left. Faced with this uncertainty, our confidence is eroding and we begin to retreat. Little by little. A little bit further into the isolated areas of our minds.

Others of us are in this rocky terrain because our deeds of the past keep us there. Our mistakes, our abuses, deeds that can't be undone, words that can't be unsaid. Jerry can't take back that affair. And Cliff can't have a do over on that deception. And we are convinced— either from our own shame or from the rejection of others—that we have made this bed and now we must lie in it.

We can even find ourselves in this isolated place through seemingly benign ways. How many of us continue to spend far more money than advisable for products promising to make our skin and our hair look more acceptable? How many more of us are injured in our weekend warrior games, trying to recapture the youth and relevance we're terrified of losing? Chasing after the youth we believe we're losing isn't just the purview of those pushing forty or fifty. It's all of us who now feel stuck by our decisions. Amanda is "only" twenty-five yet feels like she has already made too many mistakes to recover. Patrick would love to be a playwright but believes his path as an accountant is already determined by the size of his college debt. It's silly of course; we can internalize these fuzzy images of us frozen in time. And at great pain or cost we will fight to remain as we once were, for good or ill.

It's the reason people can lose enormous amounts of weight and be validated by everyone around them, but on the inside they still see themselves as needing to lose more. Still shackled by the image the mirror used to show. Still unresolved to themselves as they really are.

How do we transform fear with hope? How do we put the past into a new future?

Seeing the Boat

The hope and future of the demoniac of the Gerasenes began when something from the outside came close. He couldn't get himself out of his own story—he needed help and it came in a peculiar way. His help was in a boat filled with foreign men who were out fishing that night. It was this boat—unexpected, unasked for, arriving in the middle of the night, in the midst of a storm—that held the possibility that his life could be different.

There is a reason why the old stories we tell ourselves are so often called *self-fulfilling prophecies*. There's a reason why the AA literature describes insanity as "repeating the same behavior yet hoping for a different result." We recognize the pattern in others immediately, but in ourselves it's a different story. It seems so much more nuanced in our own lives, doesn't it? We rationalize a small shift, a change in words, a difference in tone. But really we continue to do the same actions and get the same results. Our own expectations keep these scripts firmly in play.

It's like this story Anne Lamott tells: A man is sitting in a bar in Alaska. He tells the bartender that he had been in a plane crash in the tundra. He was trapped in the wreckage and unable to get free. He began to pray for God to rescue him. He prayed and prayed and prayed. Hour after hour, nearly freezing to death. But God, he says, "didn't lift a finger to help me." The man downs a shot from the glass in front of him and says, "So I'm done with that whole charade." He decided he could never believe in a God who would treat a person like that.

But the bartender says, "You're here! You *were* saved!"

"Yeah," said the man. "But only because a group of Eskimos came along and saved me."[1]

This is the way it is. We can ask and wonder and pray. Repeatedly. Then we wonder why God doesn't answer us. The "answer" is staring us in the face, but we don't recognize it because it doesn't come in the ways we expect.

I've lost a job—so what I need is another job.

I'm lonely—so what I need is a lover. A girlfriend. A boyfriend.

My parent, my friend, my spouse is in pain—so what they need is an end to the pain.

We know the answer! This is what help looks like! This is what deliverance looks like for me!

What we most certainly do not say is: *I'm sick and confused and alienated. What I need is a boat filled with foreign guys.* That is an unexpected answer.

We have selective vision, filtering our idea of reality based on our experiences, our biases, our fears. There is a vast range of experiences and realities we encounter that we simply *do not see*. Therefore, we don't engage with them. Not only do we simply not see what is around us on a regular basis, human perception repeatedly tells us that we see what we expect to see. (Just check out some of the research on why eyewitness testimony is so unreliable.)[2]

The step of drawing hope out of our fear requires us to set aside our expectations of what's next. We have to lift our eyes toward the places, the people, the possibilities that, unconsciously or not, we have avoided seeing.

Meeting the Boat

The unexpected nature of new life is a theme that shows up over and over again throughout the Hebrew Scriptures and the stories of Jesus and his disciples. Hope comes from a source beyond our own resources. Hope is something we receive, not something we do. And generally speaking it's something so unexpected and so unfamiliar to our experiences that if we aren't careful, we will miss it.

In the Gospel of John one particular story stands out as an example of how expectations can get in the way of seeing reasons for hope right in front of us (John 4:3-29). This woman has had a hard-scrabble life. She had lost five husbands either through death or divorce. She had an existence so lonely and so marginalized that she didn't dare socialize or travel, even with other women. And her current partner—it would be saying too much to call him a "lover"—was taking advantage of her by having her live as his concubine, not good enough to marry. But she's still standing. That in itself is pretty impressive. So far, it has all the makings of a country song.

Interestingly, this woman's story sort of tells the story of her people as well. We're told that she is of mixed descent, one of the original "left behinds." Like her, her people were still standing, against all odds. The Assyrian army had defeated the kingdom of Israel and had carted off anyone who was valued by society—the craftsmen, the cultured, the skilled—to enhance the Assyrian educated class. Those left behind were the truly undesirable. They were at the bottom rungs and had nothing to offer the powerful, conquering nation. Imagine being regarded as so unimportant—so irrelevant—that an invading army can't even be bothered with you. Over time other undesirables joined this underclass. Refugees mainly.

These disenfranchised and disempowered people had Jewish blood, but because their ideas and culture had been so adulterated over the years they had become known as a separate people: the Samaritans. (Some of their descendants are still alive today in the northern and western Israel along the borders of Syria and Jordan.) The pure Jews of the south hated their former siblings for intermingling; they refused to even touch the utensils or bowls that these people had used for cooking or eating. Pure-blooded Jews wouldn't walk through Samaritan land. They wouldn't even call out to them in greeting.

Most important, for the Samaritans, their God, Yahweh, had stopped talking to them. We have no surviving religious texts from this culture from roughly the time of Moses until almost two thousand years later when Jesus encounters this woman in John's Gospel.

That's a long time of silence. Amazingly, the Samaritan people never stopped hoping. They never stopped watching for "the Christ." They never stopped believing he was going to come. To them. And they would experience a new hope so palpable that it would be like living water.

So when John writes this story of a Samaritan woman, in many ways he is writing the story of her people, alienated and written off as hopeless. He describes this surprising encounter between the waiting, parched Samaritan woman and the man who had what she most longed to receive. And yes, she almost missed him. It's the irony of life, isn't it?

She didn't recognize Jesus as anything special as he was slumped against the well. No doubt she was startled; only outcasts come to the well in the heat of the day.

She didn't recognize him when he told her he was thirsty and asked for a drink. Astonished. (*Why are you talking to me?*) Surely, this Jew didn't intend to have his lips touch the pail hers had touched.

She didn't recognize him when Jesus responded with a coy hint at his identity saying, "If you knew . . . who it is that asks you for a drink, you would have asked him and he would have given you living water" (NIV).

But she was intrigued. Excited. *Maybe he's a great teacher—possibly even greater than Jacob?* But still she didn't recognize him.

Now imagine this scene: She's waiting on a rescue, hoping for the Christ. The Messiah. Jesus arrives and has the longest conversation with any woman in all of Scripture. And still she doesn't recognize who she's talking to until after she comes clean about who she is and the reality of her life. The truth of her situation. Until she articulates those things she longs for and wishes were different, until she tells the truth and allows the stranger to tell the truth as well, she couldn't recognize Jesus for who he was and what he could do for her.

Something had to die in that woman in order to recognize and to receive what Jesus offering her. "Sir, give me a drink. Give me some of this living water." *Give me something that will stay with me, that will keep me alive, that will displace this fear and anxiety I'm living with.*

But Jesus' answer speaks an awesome truth to the woman. Jesus' answer is that living water comes very close to being deadly water. *Yes, you may drink of this water, but this water will show you the truth about yourself and the truth about your world. That truth may overwhelm you. It may come close to killing you with its clarity.*

But it is alive. It is alive with spirit and truth. It's living water.

That describes why we don't drink this living water very often. Because it's dangerous. Bringing hope into our fear involves death. This is what all the great religious traditions tell us, but still we long to squirm out of it. We want just enough living water to soothe our parched throats. We want only enough spring water to refresh us, to take the edge off. But we don't really want water enough to kill our old way of life and give us a brand new one. That's a little bit much, we think. Just a little turn of the dial is what we're after. A little satisfaction is what we want, not wholesale change.

This is the biggest, the most fundamental reason that we don't live the lives we really want. We think we just need our old ones tweaked.

But if we are to believe the one who is offering us life, then we have to believe that there is no mixing of new wine into the old wineskin carriers. There is no point in sewing a new patch on the old garment. There is no value in adding a glass of fresh water into our well of stale water.

We can't hold on to our old priorities and perspectives if we really want something to change for us.

Methodist bishop William Willimon once gave a good example of this principle. A student and professor were having one of those largely theoretical conversations that is common in seminary classes. This one concerned the question *How much water does one need for a valid baptism?* The professor looked at the student seriously, put down his pen and said, "As much water as it would take to drown in."

This is what Jesus knew: the creation of a new person, the creation of a new life, the beginning of a life you actually *want* to live as opposed to the life you are living—this involves the pain of death. Dying to old desires, old lifestyles, old patterns, old expectations.

Most of us choose to hold on to fear instead. Death is just too high a price tag.

It wasn't too high for the woman at the well. And it wasn't too high for the man living among the tombs in the region of the Gerasenes. Unlike the woman at the well, this man goes with intention to find who this strange man in the boat is.

Read the fourth chapter of the Gospel of Mark. When Jesus and his friends arrive onshore, they are weary. Jesus himself arrived exhausted. So tired he had tried to get some sleep on the way over—even during the storm with the waves pitching the boat and the thunder barreling, until his disciples shook him awake.

Jesus doesn't go looking for anyone. It's the demoniac who takes the initiative to get to the Son of God. He recognizes something is unique about that boat. And in ways unexplainable from the text he realizes a power, a divinity, a signal of hope in that boat, and he chooses to take a risk. He takes a step toward it. I suspect the man himself couldn't quite explain the attraction, except that *he knows*. He has placed some faith in the possibilities, and now he is no longer focused on any risk to himself; he's focused on the one who was on that unexpected boat.

He goes out to meet the boat. Even though it is clear from the beginning of the encounter that this will be life altering. Life transforming. The demoniac realizes that it will require pain that will be akin to torture.[3] Very literally in this story there is a death involved. All the habits, the jealousies, the evil, the thwarted desires and greed and self-ambition—all of them are drawn out of the man. Along, I suspect, with the ego protections and defense mechanisms and self-absorption.

This encounter cost the demoniac his former life.

When we are undone, everything must change.

The Mystery of Transformation

In both these stories there was a deeper movement than what is observable on the outside. Something shifted inside the Samaritan woman and the delivered demoniac before there was evidence outside.

If we are going to move toward hope, then the dynamic must begin inside of us. Hope must be born in the same interior center that brought forth fear.

I once heard Richard Rohr, a Franciscan priest and writer, illuminate the difference between living from the center and living from the circumference.[4] Imagine a circle. Along the perimeter of that circle is where the activities of our lives take place. This is our "skin," the place where we take the kids to dance classes, go to the beach and meet others. This is the circumference. But the activities we *do* aren't who we are. Who we are—our identity—resides in the center. The center is our "inner castle" in the language of Teresa of Ávila.

These are the two dimensions of our lives: inner core, outer circumstances. Rohr describes us as "circumference people." What he means is that most of us live on the shallow boundaries of our lives—along the edges. We can remain on the perimeter so long that we mistake the *edges* for the *essence* of life. For many of us God remains out here along the edges.

When the apostle Paul is explaining the power of new life in Christ to a group of people in the city of Colossae, he begins by telling them clearly what the power *isn't*. The focal point of Christ's power isn't found out on the circumference of our lives; that's where the rules are found, but that's not where the power of transformation is found (see Colossians 2:16-23).

On the edges is where we find what I would call "will-power Christianity." Or, in the language of Colossians, it's where the rules live. "Why, as though you still belonged to the world, do you submit to its rules," Paul asks, "'Do not handle! Do not taste! Do not touch!'?" This is a laundry list of behaviors. It's what some of us have mistaken for the power of God.

Our churches have been really good at setting up new laws, feeding us with the expectation that if we obey the laws then new life will follow. Different churches have different rules. I used to fall into the habit that prayer had to be done in a certain way—on my knees, perhaps, or first thing in the morning. Somehow, as I let myself drift out to the edges, I imagine God will take me more seriously if I act a certain way.

A lot of us keep falling into the groove of "Good Work" or Karma laws. We believe that our nice deeds somehow cancel out our not-so-nice words of a few minutes earlier. Like God will see that and say, "Hey, she's not so bad." We know it's irrational, but we all do it to some degree. It's like we are warding off the wrath of God with a charm.

Living in the power of God is not living in a system of dos and don'ts. Not that there isn't a place for rules that help us to protect and respect one another. But Paul knew intimately that the power of God is not necessarily found in following the rules. We don't need to make changes out on the circumference. We need something that goes much deeper if we are going to live from this new identity of Christ within, this God power within.

Although I'm using the example of religious practices, those aren't the only behaviors that can keep us out here on the circumference of our lives. If we fail to consciously attend to it, we can live our entire life out there, wading ankle-deep in our own lives. Our pain, our anxieties, hurts, disappointments, betrayals—we experience them all out on the circumference, and that is where they stay.

We have to continuously pull our experience of life away from the edges and into the center, to the essence of who we are and who we long to be. It's a continual movement between the center—the internal reality of Christ within—and the external reality of not having enough time or job insecurity or our anxieties, and all the rest of it.

This distance between the core and the circumference is the ground for transformation. This is where our thirst meets that reservoir of living water.

Or as Paul wrote, this is where life and the mystery of transformation happens. This is where our experience meets the power of "Christ in you, the hope of glory" (Colossians 1:27).

St. Francis said we grow in two ways, either by prayer or by pain. We move closer to the center as a result of one of those two motivations. We may move because the center is filled with such love that we are continually drawn to it. Or we may move because the edges of the circumference are filled with such pain that we can't bear to remain there.

Have you ever thought about your life in this way? Have you ever distinguished the difference between who you really are and this exterior edge you live on? To make this movement from edge to center requires we face the reality of the edge clearly. Name the reality that *is*, not the reality you wanted it to be. That was the moment of the Samaritan woman naming her real circumstances. We must be clear about this. The movement to the center demands that we tell the truth about the exterior.

Jesus ministered in this realm. He was always asking the uncomfortable questions, setting the stage for people to acknowledge the truth of their lives. He didn't allow people to hide behind the "right" answers or pretend they had faith when they had none. He helped them see that the starting point for the power of God to work was in the place of simply accepting the reality of their lives.

For a number of years I lived close to a wonderful family with six children. They lived in a small, very modest two-bedroom, one-and-a-half bath home (with a small study, as one of their sons pointed out). It was tight. Cramped. The kids would complain about how the tight shower schedule forced them to get up earlier and earlier; their mom, a nurse, would sometimes come home late only to get up by 4:30 the next morning to get her own shower in before the day began. Everyone in the family could see they should—and could— do something about the family's physical needs. Everybody, that is, but the dad. The dad who had a plan that called for a new workroom but not a new bathroom. A dad who was working such an aggressive savings plan that he couldn't see what saving was "costing" them. A dad whose inflexibility distanced himself from the reality of what the rest of his family was living in.

No glib answers will help us move inward from on the edges. In fact, that's exactly what will get in the way first. And that's true for all of us—those who have lived a religious life and those who haven't thought about God. Ever. There is no hiding behind platitudes. There is no *Life is peachy since I accepted Jesus into my heart.* Jesus didn't have time for that stuff. So his friend Martha could say, *I'm ticked off that my sister sits here listening to you and isn't helping me cook the dinner.* And only when she acknowledged *that* reality could she hear Jesus taking her deep to the center, helping her ask herself, *Martha, have you lost sight of what's really important?* (Luke 10:38-42).

The Gospel writers record story after story of Jesus moving through lives, turning individuals' heads around to see—to own—what was really happening with them. He showed them their shame (as with the woman at the well). He showed them their pain and anger (as with the sisters of Lazarus at their brother's grave). And he showed them their fear (as his own disciples panicked in stormy seas). In each encounter, before the Jesus demonstrated his power, these people faced their reality. They named their reality.

So acknowledge what is really happening. Don't be willing to waste time blaming it on someone else or insisting it's not really happening or putting some kind of spin on it. Don't waste any more energy denying and hiding and pretending. Life is short, and there's too much at stake in this transformation. Accept the *real* reality of your life, exactly where it is. God doesn't want to hear what we think God wants to hear. God wants to hear what is. God is ready to stand with you right there in the midst of it. Right there in the center of yourself.

You do have a deeper center. Just as certainly as I do. We are *imago Dei*—the image of God. When we turn to face ourselves, we begin to move to the center where we can see God.

That center is the beginning of our new life. Facing the demons that plagued him was the beginning of new life for the demoniac. "He came to himself," the text says, and he calmly began listening to the teaching of Jesus. When Jesus got up to leave, the now-former demoniac begged to be able to leave his land and pick up a new identity in a foreign place. But Jesus said no. Instead, Jesus directed him to "Go home to your friends and tell them how much the Lord has done for you." That's just what the man did.

Part Two

Rediscovering Trust

7

The Risk of Trust

My family had a family reunion in the Florida panhandle—close to the town of Seaside, where the movie *The Truman Show* was filmed. Walking around Seaside, I recalled some of the fictional town of Seahaven, where Truman, played by Jim Carrey, lived. As the movie starts, we see that Seahaven is a pleasant, peaceful, ocean-front town (as is Seaside). Truman Burbank lives an idyllic life. Perfect really. It's perfect of course because it's all fabricated. His friends are all being played by actors. Truman's wife only pretends to love him, his colleagues are reading scripts, the set designers are daily constructing his reality. His life is fiction, and Truman is the only one who doesn't know this.

A magazine picture of a girl he once loved (a former actress who had left the show) awakens something in Truman and the rest of the film centers on how he tries to escape from this untroubled dream world of Seahaven and into the uncertain real world that lies beyond.

Truman encounters obstacles placed in his way: choreographed traffic jams, sudden car breakdowns, a nonexistent nuclear meltdown and an artificially created hurricane on a fake ocean. Truman has to leave the security of all that he knows in order to experience real life. We do too.

Being honest about who we are is a huge step. But it's preliminary. The next challenge is to actually live in the risk and vulnerability that trusting God and others demands.

Into the Abyss

It is pretty spectacular that Abraham chooses to place his trust in God's bigger-than-life promises; as a risk-taker he is almost without exception. Almost, but not quite. I know this is all subjective, but personally I've had a particular fondness for a man who often is underappreciated: Joseph, the carpenter, who steps out in a big way when he finds out that his fiancée is pregnant. *By God!* (See Matthew 1:18-25.)

An angel breaks the news: "Joseph, son of David, do not be afraid to take Mary as your wife, for the child conceived in her is from the Holy Spirit." Talk about being undone! Talk about it's "the end of the world as we know it." Joseph is often described as a "righteous" man. For a Jewish man of that period, righteous looked like being really good at keeping all the expected behavior of the laws. Joseph was a rule-abiding man. He knew the rules for what food to eat and what clothes to wear. He knew the rules for atoning for his sins and the rules for honoring his parents. And he knew the rules for what should happen when a woman was pregnant by anyone other than her husband. She is supposed to be brought forward for a public trial. The rules were pretty simple. If the woman was raped, then she could live. If she had been complicit in sleeping with another man, she and the man would be—*should be*—stoned to death.

But Joseph was a direct descendant of God's friend Abraham. He knew the heart of God that was behind those rules—a heart of mercy and love. Joseph also knew God's rules for living justly and kindly. And Joseph, "a righteous man and unwilling to expose [Mary] to public disgrace, planned to dismiss her quietly." As Matthew describes it in his Gospel, Joseph was going to do the right thing by divorcing her, but he would do it tenderly, sensitively. Not in a public trial but by quietly nullifying their engagement.

It's at this point that a boat pulls up along the shore—just as unexpectedly as the boat came for the demoniac in the last chapter. This time the boat comes in the form of an unbidden dream.

In the dream God approaches Joseph with a proposal: *Joseph, I'm breaking all the rules of what being right looks like. I'm breaking all the rules of expected behavior, Joseph. And I'm asking you—you just man, you righteous man—to believe in something not yet seen, to have assurance of things that have only been hoped for, so that in this moment—in your lifetime—a virgin will bear a son, whom the world will call Emmanuel, God with us. Not only am I breaking the rules, Joseph, but I'm asking you to break them with me—on faith. Are you with me?*

I expect the question hung in the air for a bit.

"The one who is righteous will live by faith," St. Paul will write more than fifty years after Joseph's dream (Romans 1:17). Whenever I read that, I'm taken to that scene in the film *Indiana Jones and the Last Crusade*, where the bad guys chase Indiana Jones (played by Harrison Ford) right to the edge of an endless chasm with seemingly no way to get across. It would take a leap of faith to get across. Indiana Jones remembers, the righteous live by faith. He pauses, then raises his foot, preparing to bring it down. He takes a breath and steps out into the air. No safety net.

Just a promise, a quote, open to interpretation. No rules. Just the sense that *I think this is what I'm supposed to do.* It's only as Indiana Jones lowers his foot and begins shifting his weight toward the chasm that the rocky staircase appears. Unseen until he commits himself to this risk and fully steps into the abyss. And there it is: a way where there once was no way.

He rushes to the other side. His life is spared.

God asks Joseph to trust—not in the concrete rules of being right but in the promise of God alone. The angel reveals God's plan to Joseph in a dream, a liminal state and asks: *Do you trust me? I'm breaking the rules. You can be a part of something bigger than you could have imagined. You could take part in this chance to save more lives that you will ever fathom.*

You don't have to stand on honor or on being right. You don't have to assert or defend your husbandly rights at Mary's expense. You can risk the whispers, the potential ridicule. You are going to live in some risk, in some uncertainty. There will be complications, grief. Things will appear gray, and you won't understand.

But you can trust me. Take Mary as your wife.

This isn't that different a message from the one Jesus delivered when he sat five thousand people down and he told his disciples to feed them. One young boy believed there would be enough food, and to prove it he shared his lunch of five fishes and seven loaves of bread.

It isn't that different a message from the one Truman encountered when the mast of his sailboat hit the paper screen of the set's backdrop, and he left the only world he had known, trusting that the immensity of the real world was better than any manmade one.

It's not that different a message from the one Jesus asked his disciples to believe as they crossed the fourteen-mile lake of Galilee when a storm whipped across the water.

Into the Storm

Growing up in Florida, you really learn a lot about tropical storms. You learn, firsthand, what kind of damage they're capable of, and you learn to take them seriously. I remember seeing how Hurricane Camille whipped our hundred-year oak trees like they were little boys. That storm took our boat dock and deposited it on the neighbor's yard. I remember how Hurricane Andrew took entire schools and houses down. I've been in a lot of storms—physical and otherwise. And I can remember one storm that, while not particularly violent, may have left the biggest imprint on me.

Central Florida is riddled with lakes, large and small. I grew up on one of those lakes and spent plenty of time on it. After school late one afternoon, a friend and I rushed out to sail on his brand new Hobie Cat. It was a small catamaran—essentially a tarp strung across two runners sitting on the water. We had been out an hour or so when the sky darkened and one of the famous four o'clock lightning storms came bearing down on us—a storm we should have known was inevitable. We were a red-and-white bull's eye sitting in the middle of a three-mile lake. Two dummies sitting inches above the water on a nylon tarp. The metal mast on our little boat was the tallest thing around, practically begging the lightning, *Strike here!* We were in the middle of a terrific storm and had no way of getting ourselves out of it.

Jesus' disciples—his friends—had also known their share of storms. Matthew, one of the disciples who did not happen to be a fisherman, conveys the sense of helpless fright during one of these storms. The lead up to this moment had been stressful.

The group had recently received word that their friend John the Baptist, a prominent leader in this new movement, had been gruesomely killed by the local Roman-appointed ruler. As soon as John's body was in the grave, his followers rushed to tell Jesus about it. *Would Jesus be next?* people wondered.

Matthew wrote that when Jesus heard the news he withdrew in a boat to a deserted place by himself (see Matthew 14). John the Baptist was more than a friend to Jesus. He was his cousin; Jesus had likely grown up with him, since they were close in age. John paved the way, baptizing Jesus himself. No wonder that after receiving the news of his cousin's death Jesus was hoping for just a moment to collect

himself, to stop for a minute and just breathe. To pray and reflect
and rest. But that was not to be. The growing crowds that had been
following them for weeks got wind of where he was and descended
on him—a storm of needs and demands.

Jesus was coming to the end of a long day of teaching, listening to
people's sorrows, healing their eyes, ears, bodies and limbs. Yet he
managed to provide one more mercy as he found the energy and power
to feed more than five thousand people who clamored after him.

But as soon as it was accomplished—"immediately," the text says—
Jesus sent the disciples on ahead to their next destination across the
lake and sent the crowd home. And once again Jesus sought out the
smallest of privacies, the most basic of desires: solitude.

The disciples set out across the lake. It should have been a quick
trip, but they found themselves in a mighty headwind, battling to
stay afloat. Any thoughts of a little downtime were sinking fast. *Hey!
We could use a little help here!* They were more than apprehensive
now. They were scared.

And that's where I often feel like I could be entering this story.

Hey, I could use a little help here!

We've all been there. Maybe you're there right now. Our little
boats, the arrangements of our lives are in danger! We're in a storm
and—*God, why won't you calm the waves?*

And here's the thing: Jesus could have stepped in and simply
stopped the storm on that night. (He had done just that thing a few
chapters earlier in Matthew's book.) But if he had, we would have
missed one of the most exciting events recorded in the Gospels. We
would have missed this moment when a bold yet frightened man
decided that he was no longer going to sit fearfully by, gripping the
side of the boat and hoping that the storm would blow over. Instead,
Peter stood up and hurled himself into the very waters that threatened
his existence. He saw Jesus on the water. He heard Jesus ask him to
come, he took a deep breath, and into the waves he went.

Without the storm Peter wouldn't have gotten out of the boat and walked on the water. Storms can be more than just a threat. They can give us more than just another "hold on for dear life!" moment. A storm can be the place where miracles happen.

So what might allow us to get out of the boat? Storms are an inevitable, unavoidable given. Things will not work out the way you thought. John gets beheaded. People are all over you with needs and demands. Bad news comes at an already bad time. The boat starts to rock just when you set out on calm seas. You get laid off. Your partner lets you down. Your dog dies. That's going to happen. And when it does, you can get paralyzed—frozen in fear and clinging to the boat.

That's right where eleven of the twelve disciples stay—in the boat. And so many times I'm one of the eleven. Whatever storm I'm in, I can be captive to the waves, to the wind and most especially to the boat that I'm traveling in. A boat that I know pretty well and one that allows me to feel pretty comfortable staying right where I am, I hunker down and determine to ride it out.

Peter was a fisherman. He defined his whole life by being in that boat. That boat was his manliness, his profession, his livelihood. Yet for the love of Jesus, he gets out of the vessel that he trusted, that kept him safe, that provided for his family, that gave him all he had.

Jesus calls him, and Peter steps out.

For the love of Jesus. For the *love* of Jesus. Peter loves something more than the safety of the boat. He loves something more than riding out the storm. It's responding to the call of his friend.

We don't get out of the boat for a thrill; we won't leave the only safety we know just for the heck of it—to try something new. We would never leave the boat of our habits, our attitudes, our plans unless we were compelled by something bigger than the storms that toss us. Love—overwhelming, unrelenting, unending love is the thing that compels us to unclasp our white knuckles from the side and jump in the waves. Peter walked on water for the love of Jesus.

I'm pretty sure Peter had no idea his jumping over the side and into the storm was going to be remembered thousands of years later. Peter had an acute sense of how small a player he was in this unfolding drama. I know that about myself as well. I know I have only a little faith. But that's all I need.

That's all you need too.

When Peter starts to sink under the water, Jesus quickly reaches to catch him, exclaiming, "You of little faith, why did you doubt?" For years I've always inserted a little *tsk, tsk* in Jesus' voice. With years to contemplate just what might be accomplished with only a little faith, now I read this passage differently. Now I read it thinking Jesus sounds more like *Way to go Peter! You didn't have a lot of faith, but you had some! That's all you need!* Peter was willing to step out on the little faith he had. Eleven others stayed right where they were.

Peter's little bit of faith sparked a small action of trust, and that small action of trust changed the course of his life.

Imagine what these little bits of faith and little actions of trust could achieve if they were unleashed in the world!

Into History

To live in a place of fundamental trust is a pressing task facing our communities right now. If we're going to move beyond the old patterns of oppression, domination and fear in our society, it's going to be by being willing to risk some trust with each other in building a common future.

The Bible is a collection of stories about God wooing humanity. Over and over, God beckons men and women into relationship with himself and with one another.

Why? Because God continues to mold a people, to build a community who could be counted on to accept the stranger, love the alien, befriend the outcast, feed and clothe those who are in need. It's the story of God continuing to intervene and create people who will be an outpost of the new kingdom. That's what God is after. A people who care for the things God cares for! People who are friends of God.

But most of us have numerous experiences—perhaps lifetimes—that tell us not to trust. Ever.

A few summers ago my teenage son and I visited my brother who works and lives in Ghana—a west coast African nation. One of our stops in that first week was a visit to the Elmina slave castle along the coast. Elmina is a smaller town a couple of hours from the city of Accra. It's largely been a fishing village through its history. The castle sits on the shoreline. Along the other side of the road the houses are not much more than corrugated tin and miscellaneous pieces of lumber. They're built along trenches of open sewers.

Ghana was a primary exit point for the slave trade, and Elmina is one of three surviving ports. Built by the Portuguese in 1482, the castle was taken over by the Dutch in the mid-1600s who then held it for the next couple of hundred years.

When we arrived at Elmina, my sister-in-law said she'd prefer to wait in the car. So I went on with my fifteen-year-old son and my two nephews, both twenty-two and very buff after working construction with my brother all summer. We joined up with a group of about twenty-five others for a two-hour tour. We were four white Americans and about twenty-one people from various West African countries. All of them young, most of them male and a good many of them openly hostile.

We went in rooms that were roughly 250 feet square that would have been the living space for as many as three hundred people. The smells of defecation and urine were overwhelming. The dank, dark caverns were nauseating. One rectangular opening about thirty or so feet off the ground offered the only sunlight and ventilation in a room where the newly captive slaves were kept, naked and chained.

To say it was horrifying doesn't do it justice.

In a chamber just a few feet from the door of the holding-tank room was another dungeonlike room with a stone opening covered by a trap door. It was an opening to a chute that looked right out into the Atlantic Ocean. From this small chute, the sickest prisoners were tied with rocks and shoved out to sink into the water below.

I would say we were half-way done with the tour when I sort of stumbled on the narrow steps and one of the young men in the group pushed me hard to the wall. I turned to him with a startled *What was that all about?* look. He stared at me long enough and hard enough to be sure I was clear about his intentions. His animosity was open and deep.

The next room we arrived at was beautiful, spacious and light-filled. Devoid of all decoration but for one verse inscribed on the wall. Psalm 122:1:

> I was glad when they said to me,
>   "Let us go to the house of the LORD!"

This was the sanctuary of the Dutch Reformed Church. This is where the governor and others working in the slave trade would come to worship every Sunday. It was directly above the torture room. Directly above the horrors they were inflicting below.

While we were listening to the guide, another young man inched his way toward me, extended his leg and brought his boot heel down hard on my toes. I was wearing sandals. I tried to get my toes out while he turned toward me and said loudly to his companion, "This is another reason why I hate white people. They come here and they look all sorry. But they really don't give a - - - -. They didn't then and they don't now."

I was furious. I wanted to strike back. *Who are you? You don't know me. You don't know anything about who I am and what I'm like. I haven't done this or anything else to you. So back off!*

I was angry. I was vulnerable. Scared. We were in the bowels of this godforsaken place. My son was simply avoiding all eye contact. One of my nephews had moved off by himself; that was starting to worry me. The hard expressions, the comments, the bullying weren't being policed or interrupted by anyone, including our tour guide. Anything could have happened, and I was powerless over the outcome.

And in that second, I remembered my husband, Terry, and I talking about what it means that one out of every four African American males between the ages of sixteen and twenty-four in Chicago will be incarcerated at some point. I remembered talking with our church secretary about her son and the tears in her eyes as she told me, "You have no idea what a twenty-year-old black man faces."

I remember Terry telling me what it feels like to go to the criminal courts building in Chicago at 26th and California. How discouraging it is to see how all the "enforcers," the attorneys, the judges are mostly white. The defendants are mostly people of color.

It was a surreal moment when all these conversations came back to me, as I stood in center of the Protestant Church—*a church in the guts of this slave fort*—feeling threatened by these men and wishing first that I had a way of fighting back. But then—wishing for a way to move forward.

There we stood in this reality. Both parties angry. Both parties misunderstood. I wanted to empathize with the suffering of the stranger, but instead I found myself defensive and feeling wronged. We were not just strangers; we were estranged.

God never intended this standoff between estranged parties. From the beginning of God's call to Abraham, the people of God were blessed to be a blessing to the world (Genesis 12:2). In fact, you could argue that encounters with strangers were simply another vehicle through which the Israelites could reveal what God is like.

From the beginning of these stories of God, when Cain, the estranged son of Adam and Eve is cast out, God provides a way of protecting him. Throughout the exodus of the nation of Israel from

Egypt, God continues to provide a way for the stranger, a way for the aliens to live, a way to thrive in the company of God's people.

Is it possible that if we as individuals began trusting God enough to do some small action that perhaps our actions could be magnified in ways that would rebuild our communities and our relationships with people estranged from one another? Could we walk on the water? Could we walk across the divides that separate us?

To do so will be risky. It will leave us vulnerable and exposed. It might feel as vulnerable as climbing out of a boat on a very stormy sea. But isn't that pretty much what Jesus is getting at? If you want to be my disciple, *follow* me.

Into Yourself

When we begin to trust God, we begin to trust that there is a deeper power at work than the old patterns that have been holding us hostage. We begin to imagine, like Joseph, that the unexpected may lead to wonderful places. Like Peter, we begin to act differently and make bold choices as our trust in God grows. We may even begin to see how our communities can behave differently and begin to create common futures. Perhaps most important, when we have a little bit of faith and a little bit of trust in acting on it, we become part of a greater story.

One of the greatest, most ordinary of people changed the course of the world. Uneducated, from a rural family that has long been forgotten, this woman, through her act of trust, altered our reality.

Artists, painters and poets have had a better sense of how to understand Mary, the mother of Jesus, than most Protestants, like me. We Protestants get a little nervous about Mary. We're never quite sure how much honor to bestow on her without having to turn in our Protestant card and exchange it for a Catholic card. Our response has been to not talk very much about Mary at all. But as an example of faith, Mary stands supreme and resplendent. In part because of her ordinariness.

A few years ago I had the opportunity to visit the Monastery of San Marco in Italy—a simple structure that has been a monastery for 620 years. The artist Fra Angelico, a fifteenth-century monk who lived there, had painted a series of frescos all around the walls of the small sanctuary for his brothers to meditate on. He paints Mary in a very different way from most of the divine art I'd seen. His painting of the Annunciation has no glittering backdrop. It's just an angel and Mary against a cream wall.

Mary is plain, unadorned, dressed in a simple off-white dress. She leans forward with a curious expression, looking deeply at the angel Gabriel. Mary seems lovely but doesn't appear to be particularly knowing or particularly holy or particularly anything special. Mary appears as if she is about to speak while Gabriel appears to wait to see what she will say.

Frederick Buechner captures this moment memorably:

> She struck the angel Gabriel as hardly old enough to have a child at all, let alone this child, but he'd been entrusted with a message to give her, and he gave it.
>
> He told her what the child was to be named, and who he was to be, and something about the mystery that was to come upon her, "You mustn't be afraid, Mary," he said.
>
> As he said it, he only hoped she wouldn't notice that beneath the great golden wings, he himself was trembling with fear to think that the whole future of creation hung now on the answer of a girl.[1]

When Luke writes the story of the birth of Jesus, he barely introduces Mary as an important figure. She receives no honorifics like her cousin Elizabeth. In the first chapter of his book, he goes on about John the Baptist's parents: *Zechariah and Elizabeth? Well, let me tell you! They are blueblood! A priest from the line of Abijah, and Elizabeth is a descendant of Aaron. Yes, that's right, Aaron the brother of Moses himself! These are some upstanding, righteous people!*

In contrast, he introduces Mary as plain—ordinary. All Luke tells us is that she is a virgin engaged to a man named Joseph from the house of David. Beyond that, he doesn't suggest that she is any different than anyone who might be reading this book. At least in moral character or attribute.

There is not one word in this story about her virtue, her worthiness, her suitability or predisposition to faithfulness. Not one word that would explain to us why God should choose her. But he did. God called to Mary and made her an offer. And the heavens waited on her response. The heavens are waiting on your response as well.

8

The Reward of Trust

*I*f removing our masks is painful, and trusting God and others leaves us vulnerable, you may be wondering: What's the payoff for all this pain?

Perfect Imperfection

One of the more dramatic stories about Jesus is the telling of how Jesus raised Lazarus from death (see John 11:1-44). The back story is that Jesus had been good friends with Lazarus and his two sisters, Mary and Martha. When Lazarus got sick, his sisters sent word to Jesus asking him to come immediately to heal their brother. Jesus delayed, and by the time he got to the house, Lazarus had already died.

Jesus asks Mary to trust him, and although she is stricken with grief and anger that Jesus had not come right away, she responds that she does trust him. It is then that Jesus goes to the tomb of Lazarus. He stands at the entrance and calls Lazarus back to life.

It's a miracle.

Lawrence was a man in our church who once wrote a little story about the funeral of his father who died when Lawrence was ten years old. As a little boy Lawrence knew the famous miracle of Lazarus. And he was sure God was going to do the same thing for his father. *Surely God didn't love his father any less than he loved Lazarus, did he?* My friend waited for the miracle to happen.

The first opportunity for the resurrection was at the viewing in the funeral parlor on Saturday evening. "How glorious this will be!" Lawrence wrote. "Hundreds of eyewitnesses to the glory of God! I sit in the funeral parlor with a perfect view to observe the reactions of people when they see my father exit the coffin like Lazarus from the grave. . . . Yet, as the evening wears on my hope for resurrection diminishes and it is time to go back home, back to my dark bedroom."

In bed that night, his faith in God's work of a miracle surged again as he thought that perhaps God was just waiting for the funeral itself. Surely that would be the better moment, Lawrence reasoned. He dressed for the funeral in expectation. Ready to witness something truly miraculous.

"The service begins . . . the words and songs come and go, a continuous stream and still no resurrection. The preacher speaks— surely this is the time, the apex of the service, the climactic moment in the symphony, the time when Jesus will call forth from heaven, 'Lazarus, come forth!' But the preacher sits down. The service is winding down and desperation fills my soul. . . . The great moment is past and Jesus did not issue the call. Daddy remains motionless in the coffin. My heart sinks. I begin to realize it is not to be."

No miracle was to be had. Which raises the question of just what is the reward of trusting in God? If there isn't some amazing payoff— some tangible miracle—then why is any of it worthwhile?

Lawrence's experience has been duplicated in a thousand different ways. In the lead-up to the Lazarus miracle, Martha articulates our own words: "Lord, if you had only been here my brother would not have died!" (John 11:21).

How many times have you found yourself thinking similar thoughts:

God, if you really cared about me, I wouldn't have cancer.

If God was really watching out for me, this wouldn't have happened to my son.

Those of religious persuasion tend to believe God should bless us because of how we have sought to be obedient. As if our behavior would be enough to convince God to bless us specially. It's the "Haven't I been good enough?" argument.

Here I am, "training up a child in the way they should go," and still he has this addiction; she has the eating disorder.

Here I am working hard for a living. Trying to be a good parent, a good husband, and yet I'm one of the thousands that lost my job last month.

And many of us move angrily into all the other ways miracles should be happening and are not. The two billion people starving, the bloody rivers of the Congo and Rwanda, the tens of thousands dead by the oppressive governments of Central America. We have a nagging thought that if God *would have only been there,* it would be different. It would have turned out better.

Tell me again how I can believe in a God who could stop all the bad stuff in the world, and doesn't. Tell me again how I'm supposed to believe in the God of miracles when I've never had one happen to me.

Or, to put it another way, are there any reasons to trust in God when our stories don't end in a miracle? When we just continue to muddle on through?

This is what I've learned about miracles: There is a reason they are called miracles. They rarely happen. In life and in the Bible. Most of the Bible, most of the time, recounts what happens when people are bumbling through life as well. The honor and the beauty of life is found not in the miracles but in the ordinariness of it all. That's where the glory of humanity is most exquisite.

One of my favorite poems is "The Man Watching" by Ranier Maria Rilke. It's about a coming-of-age scene found in the book of

Genesis. After more than ten years of absence, Jacob is about to meet his older brother, Esau. The last time the brothers had seen each other Esau promised to kill Jacob. Now God has told Jacob to return home. At enormous personal risk Jacob is doing just that. The night before he meets Esau, Jacob faces a mysterious angel, and the two wrestle through the night. Jacob comes away with a debilitating limp. Hardly a miracle, but an honorable struggle. Rilke captures the nobility of the effort:

> What we choose to fight is so tiny!
> What fights with us is so great!
> If only we would let ourselves be dominated
> as things do by some immense storm,
> we would become strong too, and not need names.
>
> When we win it's with small things,
> and the triumph itself makes us small.
> What is extraordinary and eternal
> does not want to be bent by us.
> I mean the Angel who appeared
> to the wrestlers of the Old Testament:
>
>   . . .
>
> Whoever was beaten by this Angel (who often simply
>   declined the fight)
> went away proud and strengthened
> and great from that harsh hand, that kneaded him as if to
>   change his shape.
> Winning does not tempt that man.
> This is how he grows: by being defeated, decisively,
> by constantly greater beings.[1]

Rilke understood that we squander our energy and our talents when we fail to commit ourselves to the bigger struggle. To trust in

God isn't to be assured of success. Instead, it is a promise that we can commit ourselves to something great, and in so doing, we can experience something powerfully both human and divine in the process of that commitment.

Freedom

Writer Philip Yancey once did a talk at my church where he said—in a rather throw-away comment—that God wasn't looking for perfection in the Hebrew Bible, God was simply looking for people willing to engage—to go toe-to-toe with him. I've thought about that comment a lot. God is looking for people to engage, to wrestle, to grapple with the big questions and the big concerns. When Jacob leaves this tussle with the angel, he goes out with a changed name: "You shall no longer be called Jacob, but Israel, for you have striven with God and with humans, and have prevailed" (Genesis 32:22-32).

Something deeply transformational went on in the night. Jacob, now Israel, goes out marked by the experience. He's marked not only with a literal limp but also by freedom. His past deeds no longer mark him in the same way. His former name, Jacob, meant "trickster." But this was no longer going to be his identity. He went toe-to-toe with God. He went toe-to-toe with his own demons perhaps; he certainly went head-to-head with his deepest fear: the fear of seeing his brother Esau again. And he prevailed.

It's freeing to watch a person wrestling with the One who is bigger than we can think or imagine. It's freeing to experience. There is a nobility that goes beyond our own self-limiting, self-defined actions.

This is the freedom young David experienced even while he was on the run from the jealous king Saul. It's while David and his group of warriors are dashing from cave to cave that he writes one of the most beloved poems ever:

The LORD is my shepherd, I shall not want.
>   He makes me lie down in green pastures;
he leads me beside still waters;
>   he restores my soul.
He leads me in right paths
>   for his name's sake.

Even though I walk through the darkest valley,
>   I fear no evil;
for you are with me;
>   your rod and your staff—they comfort me.

You prepare a table before me
>   in the presence of my enemies;
you anoint my head with oil;
>   my cup overflows.
Surely goodness and mercy shall follow me
>   all the days of my life,
and I shall dwell in the house of the LORD
>   my whole life long. (Psalm 23)

These are the words of a free man. This is the life of a free man. That's what Psalm 23 is describing. It's a life found in God, and it's a life that David found *not* while things were going well, but as they were ostensibly terrible. This is a life that is found in God: a life that knows the rocks and the caves, but dwells by still waters and green pastures, a life generous enough to invite our enemies to the table with us, a life that rests, that celebrates, that loves even while living in the shadow of all the big mountains of death. There are so many mountains of death in our culture: disease, starvation, oppression and torture. And there are the smaller death shadows: our hurriedness, our overcommitment, our fatigue. We want that life of freedom. Even amidst the mountains of death that surround life, our table is set before us.

That life begins with us accepting the invitation. It begins with recognizing a freedom that already suffuses the world. Our only responsibility is to notice this existing freedom. To recognize and mark it. This is one reason why Jesus comes on the scene declaring, "The kingdom of God is in your midst!" (Luke 17:21 NIV).

This was the freedom God desired for people right from the beginning. This shalom life was tied to the Ten Commandments, when God instituted the creation of a sabbath rest. But the origin of the shalom life is linked to something a little different at the close of the Torah. In the book of Deuteronomy the people are coming close to the Promised Land (see Deuteronomy 5). As a society the Israelites are about to stop being a nomadic tribe and are going to settle down. As individuals they are about to start building homes, taking wives, making babies, developing customs. They are going to plant vineyards, grow crops and milk their cattle. And in between all of their daily life, they are going to establish a settled country. They will wage war and make peace, create laws, forge alliances, and build an economy.

A lot of things were going to tie them down, bind them. They were going to experience worries that could enslave them again. They would approach windows of power that could ensnare the ambitious among them and trap the weak. So God gives them the law again, but this time he doesn't talk about resting after creation. This time, God connects it to freedom. "Remember that you were a slave in the land of Egypt, and the LORD your God brought you out from there with a mighty hand and an outstretched arm" (Deuteronomy 5:15). In sabbath living, you remember you are not a slave anymore.

I'm not a slave anymore. Not to my ambition. Not to my insecurity. I'm not enslaved to my pride. To my secret sins. To my financial worries. To any of my longstanding fears.

I am free.

The Power of Change

But the shalom life does require changes. Only they aren't those will-power kind of changes that we can make happen. The changes required by the shalom life are more of the receptive variety. It's not about making changes; it's about being changed. And being willing to take the hit for changing when it does happen. One of the most important aspects of change is simply being strong enough to hold on to it in the wake of criticism. I've learned as a pastor that if you want everybody to like you, then don't do too much. Oh, I mean, sure, visit the sick, comfort the lonely. But don't actually try to make some changes. Because as soon as you want to make changes somebody is soon barking about how much power you have while another has gone on overload scanning the church bylaws to tell you why change is against the rules.

The Gospel of John tells a story about change that seemed to set everyone's teeth on edge. Some say that it sets in motion the unfolding chain of antagonism that will culminate at the cross.

The story opens with a blind man sitting by the side of the road (John 9:1-34). It wasn't a particularly rare occurrence in the ancient world for the blind, poor and lame to sit alongside the main roadways hoping for some coins. Day after day the man sits there begging—largely unnoticed, part of the landscape. The drama starts when Jesus passes by the blind man, and instead of doing the expected thing Jesus stops and listens and heals. The man begins to see. That's when the dam breaks lose. As long as everybody is playing the roles they have scripted for themselves, then there's no controversy. But let somebody get well and it's a different story completely.

Psychologists often talk about systems theory. The theory proposes that families or organizations of any kind tend to operate like a single emotional unit, made up of interlocking parts. When one part changes, the whole system is affected. The other parts have to adapt to that change. When we change as individuals, we can expect some push back from the systems we participate in.

Just like the blind man who begins to see. Now all the people around him must change. And the truth is that there are always plenty of reasons why we do not want to change.

All of us are captive to the patterns of our behavior. And most of us are captive to the behaviors of those we live with or work with. Some of our patterns are dark and only known to us privately. They are those things we nurse. We protect those patterns, almost refusing to believe it could be otherwise. Other patterns are more public.

As a good friend, an internist, tells me, until the pain of staying as you are is greater than the pain of changing, a patient simply won't change. We will continue to smoke, to drink, and to eat our way right into the grave unless and until the pain of continuing that way of life is greater than the pain and loss we face when we stop it.

Maybe you're one of those people who has a habit that's hard to change, so you know what I'm talking about. Or maybe you read this and shake your head about those other people who can't control themselves. As for me, it's been remarkably easy for me to under-estimate my reluctance to change.

One of the greatest, most decisive men in the Hebrew Bible had trouble changing. I derive a lot of hope from that. His story gives some complexion to how we may go about finding a sense of freedom and trust amid the fear in our own lives as well.

Samuel is one of the wisest counselors and prophets recorded in Israel's history. It was a transitional time in Israel's history. God had first declared that the nation of Israel would be without monarchs, which set it apart from other nations. Instead, through the voice of prophets, God had instituted a government through which people would observe the decrees of a series of judges. But the people of Israel (no doubt uncomfortable with uncertainty and the ongoing changes in leadership) clamored for a monarch. God heard them and acquiesced. The era of being ruled by judges was over. With the coronation of the first king, Saul, a new era in Israel's history had begun: the reign of kings.

Unfortunately the reign of Saul goes south in a hurry. After an initial flurry of hope and excitement, it is clear that something needs to happen to get Saul out of office. The prophet Samuel is stuck with the job of informing Saul that God has rejected him as king. This rejection is an important detail that for several years only Samuel and Saul will know.

Samuel delivers the news to Saul in 1 Samuel 15, laying out the various reasons God wants Saul to step down: Good people have behaved badly. Bad choices have been made. The optimism and hope that the monarchy might bring leadership and direction is now dashed. King Saul is exposed as the doomed Ozymandias of Percy Bysshe Shelley's poem.[2] He is a colossal wreck, weak to the opinions of others, a liar who will become increasingly unstable.

After Samuel delivers the news, both men return to their homes and don't see each other again until the day Samuel dies. Saul goes home to continue to wear his mask of "kingliness." (After all, no one else knows.) But Samuel goes home in sorrow over this wretched state of affairs. He's angry; he's grieving over the failed situation, the failed Saul, the floundering hope. And the great prophet—this man who time and again has proceeded with decisive action—starts to check out. Shut down. Disengage.

We don't know how long this state of grief, lethargy, passivity, helplessness lasted. But after some window of time, God comes to Samuel and asks, "How long will you grieve over Saul?"

How long are you going to sit here staring out the window of your house here in Ramah?

How long are you going to nurse the wounds of the past? How long are you going to weep for a lost hope? A previous moment? How long are you going to keep doing this? Wishing and wistful for a past dream that is not going to happen? How long are you going to think the same thoughts, do the same things over and over as though you expect it will lead to a different result?

I have rejected him from being king over Israel. It's over. Come to grips with that, Samuel. Now get up. Get some supplies ready. I'm sending you to Jesse who lives outside of Bethlehem, for I have provided for myself a king among his sons.

I recognize well the wisdom of the dictum: The definition of insanity is doing the same thing over and over and expecting a different result.

In various ways this is what's happening when we resist change itself. We want our lives to be different, but we keep doing the same things—even while longing for some new result from the very same actions and patterns.

How long will we . . . is the question my husband and I finally asked ourselves when we thought that if we would just scream louder and slower, our son would begin to do better in school. What we were doing was not working. And the answer was not to keep doing the same thing. The answer was to find whether there was a new approach. A fresh understanding. A way of looking at reality through a different set of eyes. But it took us years to get to that question. Years.

More painfully, I know a woman whose husband has carried on an affair for several years. For the last two years or so she has known about it. But until recently she could not confront it. Although she has agonized and wept and grieved over it, she couldn't move past her wish that it just wasn't happening. At one point I might have found her avoidance to be extreme, but now I know better. I hear too many stories where the pain of confronting reality is simply too difficult.

There are things we universally avoid: How long will we continue to overwork to prove to ourselves that we may, in fact, be able to silence that voice that tells us we are only as good as what we produce? How long will we continue to grip the past like it's our lifeline, resisting the inevitable pull of the future?

How long? I would suggest that it will go on as long as it continues to work for us. As long as it continues to be the justification we use, the reason we can blame, the story that continues to define our lives and keeps us from change.

As a friend of mine once said, We build an endoskeleton around the hurts, the wounds. That's our spine, our structure, the narratives we tell, the scripts we follow, because that's what we know. That's our experience.

And here's the real payoff: We paradoxically give ourselves and keep ourselves in power by continuing in the world we've created. We know what the outcome will be. We control it! So we do it over and over and over again.

Faithfulness

Ultimately what God promises when we take the risk to trust is nothing less—and nothing more—than himself. God's presence, God's power, God's patience, God's peace, God's very self. That's what is promised us as we slowly release our white knuckles as they cling to our fears and habits. That's what we find when we become more alive to God's shalom life around us and in us.

But in order for that presence to be manifest, it has to seep into every area, every crevice of our lives. This is the thing about God our churches don't describe very well. As long as we are patching a few things here and there, we will miss the transformational joy God wants us to experience. We may add this habit or that belief, tacking them on to our existing proclivities, but we miss the overall meaning these habits and beliefs are pointing us too.

One of the most memorable examples I have of this comes from the Tim Burton film *The Nightmare Before Christmas*. The main character is a scarecrow with a removable skull head: Jack, the Pumpkin King.

Jack's the most famous citizen of Halloween Town—a place of perpetual Halloween, all in black and white, with scary tricks and fiendish ghouls. "Where people trick or treat until the neighbors die of fright."

But one day Jack stumbles into the world of Christmas Town. He's completely intrigued by what he finds there. All the little things he finds in Christmas Town seem so happy, so fun. It's a world completely foreign to Jack. He simply can't understand what he sees.

Jack doesn't know. He doesn't know why children get candy canes instead of black spiders in their beds; he doesn't know why people are singing and the presents are pretty. *But he likes the way it makes him feel.*

So he snatches the stocking, the mistletoe, the trees with little lights, the presents; he even snatches Santa himself. He hauls them all back to Halloween Town, where he and his ghouls begin pasting these trappings onto his Halloween life.

They happily fill the wrapped boxes with shrunken heads. They hang the Christmas stockings with a foot still in them. They decorate the trees with spiders and hide under the bed to scare the children senseless when they wake up excited on Christmas morning.

As you can imagine: It's a disaster.

Jack has all the trappings—but he doesn't know the deeper meaning of what's going on. He has the objects, but he has missed the point of it all.

Often in matters of faith and spirituality, we take stuff from here or there and patch it on. We take the trappings of Christianity and we patch them on, because just as it worked for a little while for Jack, it feels pretty good to us. Sometimes. Sort of.

We get into a bad spot and we find ourselves praying. (And that's a good thing.) We do something we can't hide anymore, and we come clean and confess. (And that's a good thing too.) We make a little contribution to a good cause, and we like the way it makes us feel generous. (Good again—the world needs this.) But we are a little bit like Jack. We don't put it all together and start to reorganize ourselves around a new way of thinking, being and living. We "get" the parts, but we miss the whole.

We're not alone in this. The earliest followers of Jesus Christ had the same problem as Jack. They kept wanting to take the parts of his teaching that they liked.

How about that part about restoring the nation of Israel! Let's hear that one again!

What about the part where us poor people will have enough to eat?

Tell me the one again about the enemies of God being destroyed!

They kept failing to see that following Jesus meant going into dangerous places; it meant doing things that seemed threatening or will make them vulnerable. It meant their pride must get in the back seat. It meant their defensiveness or their perceived wrongs, even the things they were right about. All must be put in service to Christ first.

It means that for us too. To really transform fear with trust, we must be the first to love. We must be the first one to forgive. The first one to open our home to others. The first one to set aside our ambition for the love of Jesus.

It also means also challenging the story we see around us—the story that says the more successful you are, the better you are. The story that says look out for yourself first. The story that follows a script set by advertisers. It means running our businesses and doing our jobs by standards of fairness, respect and honesty that trump the bottom line.

There's nothing piecemeal about that at all. It's a full-out life adjustment. An adjustment that will ask for everything.

9

What Does
God Want from Me?

I was well into my early thirties before I began to believe God wasn't hunting me for sport. The big eye in the sky was everywhere—the Bible told me so. God knew when I woke up and when I went to sleep. This used to freak me out. It was creepy and a little bit terrifying to imagine someone watching every little thing. Nowhere to hide? No actions, ideas, emotions that I could hold privately? I remember my new Christian friends would try to tell me I should feel reassured, not threatened. "This is good news!" they would exclaim. Really? Because I have to tell you, generally I felt like a babysitter on a nanny-cam. I felt I was being judged, ranked and evaluated on every action. I suppose if you were from a Roman Catholic background, you might imagine the familiar image of the nun with the ruler. Since I wasn't, I just envisioned a very stern military man. Exacting. Demanding. Oh yes, there was also a divine soft side, which could be activated by my very sincere repentance. But even God's forgiveness wasn't all that comforting since I could never really be sure I was truly repentant. These questions vexed me: Was I *really prepared* to turn from anger? From gamesmanship? From revenge? Just how big a blanket was divine forgiveness after all?

There was one way I could prove to God how serious I was about repentance and discipleship. That was by drafting my own set of rules complete with its categories of rewards and punishments. So, for example, if I was sarcastic to someone, I would go without sugar the next day. Or if I had gossiped, I would, for example, deny myself the pleasure of going to the movies.

This "sin chart," as I called it, became my personal accountability system. My grid informed me about how much goodness I deserved. How much pleasure and abundance I should allow myself. All the things God didn't seem to be telling me. It could tell me where divine patience might be wearing thin.

Weird. I know. Worse than weird, this whole system was destroying the little amount of love and desire I did believe God had for me.

It took a lot of years before I talked about my sin chart openly. And when I did, I realized plenty of others were living from an understanding of what they "deserved." Self-loathing, I found, is rampant, manifesting itself in all-out recklessness on the one hand (*I'll do what I want, when I want, with whomever I want!*), to my proclivity for ascetic-like self-denial (*I don't deserve forgiveness!*) on the other. They look different on the outside, but they both are reactions to the same inner core: I've been sized up and found wanting. I careened between both positions until I started reflecting seriously on what God might actually want for me. For us.

The Gospel writer Luke records an *aha* moment that happened with a woman I can readily identify with. The story is set in a Jewish synagogue—a building that was, by its very construction, intended to keep people segmented. Where you sat in the synagogue communicated just where you stood vis-à-vis God. (*An architectural sin chart?*) The area for the priests was close to the front. Jewish men sat behind them. Jewish women were in the back. And the Gentiles stood out in the courtyard. Each group separated by a wide berth of space.

Every day, people of all sorts came here to teach and be taught. They came to repent, to beseech, to grieve and to get a glimpse of One who was greater than they. People came to experience something of a glory, a purpose, a manifestation beyond themselves. The one they called Jehovah.

Into this scene in Luke's Gospel shuffles a woman, utterly disabled (see Luke 13). Bent over completely, the text says. When I imagine this woman, I think of the hunched-over older women throughout the developing world. I've seen women in this condition throughout China and Japan. Caused by a blend of a diet lacking calcium and a lifetime of carrying everything on their backs. This woman's condition was even worse than what it seemed.

Like the fall leaves that curl and twist closed, this woman is crippled completely. The cultural and religious understanding would place the blame on her. It was her sin weighing her down. Who knew all the secrets she had carried, her hidden actions that lived in her and weighed her down and over? The pain and the humiliation would have been unrelenting and unending.

Stop and imagine this. When was the last time she had been able to look up and see the trees? Had it been decades since she had felt the hot sun on her cheeks? Or the wind in her face? Had it been years since she had seen anything but her feet? Her feet. Dirty and sore. If the woman saw anything, she saw it sideways, distorted and disoriented.

We know nothing about her faith. Nothing about her life. Nothing other than the fact that she had come to the synagogue.

She comes to the synagogue on a day when Jesus is teaching.

She doesn't approach Jesus. From her spot near the back, she most likely can't even see Jesus. No. It is Jesus who calls out to her. "Woman, come over here."

I imagine her being paralyzed with fear. Was she going to be yet another object lesson? Another opportunity for a religious leader to say, *This—this is what happens for those who disobey!* Yet another occasion to say, *I'm sorry! I'm so sorry!* Was she going to be chastised for not worshiping enough or not giving enough?

Remembering my sin chart, inspired by my own self-doubt, I've wondered if she was worried about having her divided, half-hearted repentance exposed.

Some of us think like that, don't we? We have that ache in our hearts that God is calling us, but we just can't go there. "Come over here!" Jesus urges. There is so much separating the woman's section from where Jesus is! To respond would mean she would have to violate the rules of the synagogue. She's not supposed to be up there with the men. She's not supposed to be up front. To obey Jesus would mean to ignore the place she's been given. After all, this is the hand she's been dealt: She's a woman, she's disfigured, she's forgettable, so marginalized she's not even named in the Gospel that tells her story.

To come to Jesus meant this woman would have to leave the back of the court of women, to shuffle though the men gathered in the court of Israel, with their eyes burning into her and their whispers following behind her, to get to the front where the teacher sat. It took a lot of guts for her to make her way to Jesus. She had to disobey some rules—the rules she lived by.

Jesus heals her, echoing words he had said at another synagogue in Nazareth, a city a few miles away: "Woman, thou are loosed!" (Luke 13:12 KJV). *You're free!* The Greek word is *apoluō*. It's not a word used very often in healings. It's a word used to untie, to release. You may *apoluō* your donkey or ox so they can graze freely.

Apoluō, Jesus says. And for the first time in eighteen years, she stands up and sees the sky. For the first time in almost two decades, she straightens her hands above her head and shouts, "Mighty is the God who has set me free!"

The reaction of this woman—being loosened from all the shame, the crippling judgment, the pain of everyday living, this intoxicating burst of liberation—*this* is what God wanted for me. First and forever. This God was the one behind freedom, mercy and abundance. After reading this scene I went back and reread the first pronouncement Jesus said about himself in the Gospel of Luke. It's his first sermon from Luke 4. Jesus picks up the ancient scroll of a Jewish prophet who lived some six hundred years earlier and reads this stirring emancipation proclamation:

> The Spirit of the Lord is upon me,
>   because he has anointed me
>   to bring good news to the poor.
> He has sent me to proclaim release to the captives
>   and recovery of sight to the blind,
>   to let the oppressed go free,
> to proclaim the year of the Lord's favor.
>   (Luke 4:18-19; see Isaiah 61:1-2)

Right now.

This is what the presence of God looks like—seen only in random gasps of recognition and wonder: It's a woman seeing the sun for the first time in decades. It's someone who has been hidden and invisible now striding to center stage. It's the moment of dignity descending like a mantle on the shoulders more accustomed to carrying the burdens of daily living. This moment of recognition, of freeing power, this "year of the Lord's favor"—this is the primary message of God to you. To me. To our world.

Everything else is supporting documentation. Ways, means and structures for how we can knowingly live in an awareness of God's favor.

But I had let those "ways and means" get in the way of the primary message.

Sort of like the synagogue leader in the Luke text, I had forgotten that the "good news" is a liberation message; it goes against the rules!

Now in general, of course, we want release for those who have been rehabilitated. And we want freedom for those who have done their time. And surely we want blind people to start taking care of themselves. And good news to the poor in the minds of some is a good thing, because it means they can get a job.

When the synagogue leader responds indignantly to Jesus liberating this woman, we might soothingly suggest he was just doing his job. His job is, after all, to teach the law—the implications of the law. And—*Sorry, there's a rule against healing today*—healing counts as work, and there's a rule against working on the sabbath.

If it had been something truly life threatening, breaking the rules might be reasonable. Like maybe saving a woman who's lying unconscious in a burning house. Okay, you can go get her out. Or say if your sheep falls into a pit on the sabbath, then you can rescue it, else it would die.

But heal a woman who has already lived eighteen years in her condition? It just doesn't meet the standard of an emergency. The indignant leader might easily surmise, if Jesus had just waited to heal the woman outside after the sabbath day was over, there wouldn't be such a fuss.

The synagogue leader could have comfortably interpreted Jesus, the Messiah miracle worker, through the rules we've all set up here: *No calling a woman into the men's area. No healing on the sabbath. There are six other days! What's the rush?*

In the synagogue leader's mind, it's Jesus who has created a crisis— by deliberately healing against the rules.

And he would be right about that. Jesus did heal that woman intentionally and without apology. In the men's-only section of the synagogue. On the sabbath. He was reframing the rules.

Jesus is determined and unshakeable from the moment of his baptism onward. Something happens to him as he emerges from the water, as the cloudy skies part to reveal a sun-drenched stream of light that rests upon him. A voice verifies the identity that was always his, but now it's revealed and validated: "You are my Son, the Beloved; with you I am well pleased" (Luke 3:21-22).

The next few years for Jesus are marked with urgency and passion. A message and a mission. And without relishing the glory of the moment, Jesus immediately goes out to ask people to realize the insight that he is aware of: The kingdom of God is here. Now. And you are part of it. Join in the story. Believe God is *for* you, and join me.

With the arrival of Jesus, everything changes. God comes walking right up to people. Now God could be anyplace, advancing anywhere. Asking anything of anyone at anytime, talking to fishermen going about their business. Striding into the bedrooms of sick mothers-in-law. Kneeling beside lepers and sick paralytics.

In Jesus, God is on the loose and asking people to come alongside and join him.

And here's what he says, *Repent! Metanoia!* The word means "change your mind." Change your mind about the way you have thought about righteousness and purity and love and war. Change your mind about the barriers you've constructed to live righteous lives. Change your mind about where you thought God dwelled and what you thought God would do and how you thought God would treat you. Change your mind about what you do and don't deserve.

Regularly, the people Jesus encountered needed to answer only one question: *Do they want to follow Jesus into the kingdom? Or not?* Jesus calls out, *The kingdom of God is here. Follow me while I show it to you. Listen to me while I describe it. Watch this life of God unfold in front of your eyes.*

I had done with my list of rules just what the religious establishment had done before me, I had made this idea of freedom — of living in God's life — into another rule to obey. But Jesus was not interested in inviting people to follow another rule. He was inviting

people to so identify with the man Jesus Christ that they would be —
that *we* would be — willing to become who we were formed to be all
along. Accepting the call to follow is accepting the call of the eternal
yes that is at the core of the universe. It's the image of a bent over
woman standing with the wind on her face and a smile on her lips.

This is the life I was after when I settled on the sin chart.

See, if we don't fully believe this reality that God is *for us* — that
Jesus is *for us* — then we will keep stumbling over what we "deserve" or
what we've "earned." After we get that straight, then we can begin to
realize the entire human experiment — our life included — is one of
lavish grace and divine favor. *The year of the Lord's favor is right now.*

Trust Yourself to the Water

On one of the last nights of his life, Jesus used a horticultural met-
aphor to convey the future to those who had chosen to follow him
in this kingdom life. "Abide in me," he says, "as I abide in you"
(John 15:4).

I used to put that phrase on my sin chart. "Abide in me." I wasn't
so sure what "abide in me" meant, but it sounded significant and it
sounded comforting. I occasionally worried it might be like some
kind of straining to be holy, and so if I hadn't been aware of actively
trying to be "good" (or as Jesus says later in this same section of text,
"bear fruit") then often I would mark another "x" indicating "need
to improve."

Now I see his statement not as prohibition but as a promise. *Trust
in my abiding love*, Jesus says. *Trust yourself to me. Trust yourself to
the water that flows from the well of life. Trust yourself to the water
and let the current take you where you need to go. The water will bear
you up and accomplish God's purposes.*

Come and abide in me as I abide in you. This is God's invitation.

Ezekiel was an early Hebrew prophet, and he used some similar
images in his prophecies. In his mind's eye Ezekiel saw a river so

wide it couldn't be crossed. A river "deep enough to swim in," and in this vision, he heard God tell him "there will be many fish, and stagnant waters will be made fresh. Wherever this river goes, everything will live" (see Ezekiel 47:58-59).

Wherever this river goes, everything will live. Trust yourself to the water. Earlier in John's Gospel, a man was given the same invitation. The sickly man spent thirty-eight years lying beside a pool, too weak to enter the pool himself. Jesus asked him, "Do you want to be made well?" (see John 5).

If you do, trust that I abide in you, trust that my presence is with you, trust me to do what I have said I will do.

"Stand up, take your mat and walk."

Trust yourself to the water, and do what would be unthinkable in your own power. Trust yourself to the water—you broken women, you exhausted men. Stand up and see the sun.

Trust yourself to the water, Peter. The great disciple had to choose whether he could do this later in John's book. His ringing declaration to Jesus, "I will lay my life down for you!" was followed by a spectacular failure. He panicked and denied he even knew Jesus when the authorities came for him. Would Peter believe that the sting of his humiliation could be soothed in that water? Would he believe that the vinelike, twisted trajectory of his life could actually be an example of God's power and grace? (See John 13 and John 18.) Jesus gave Peter some excellent teaching on betrayal, arrogance and failure. But Peter didn't understand what Jesus was talking about until he actually betrayed Jesus. Peter's failure was the impetus for his understanding and maturity. *Peter, abiding with me is not based on your ability to keep a keep a good sin chart! It's about trusting that I've got you no matter what.*

This is what I've learned in the years since my sin chart. That abiding and trusting often look like wading back out into the water again. Thinking of myself and my failures less—and thinking about

God's love more. *Abide in me as I abide in you.* It frees us from the "oughts" but not from the pain and loss associated with life. Jesus is ever the realist.

The rocks in the riverbed are still going to hurt.

On occasion I've gone whitewater rafting. There are times when you're paddling like crazy and times when you're bored. Then there are times when it seems like no matter which way you paddle, no matter how hard you paddle, the river is carrying you right into that huge boulder in the middle of the stream. Right where you didn't want to be.

One of the last things that Peter hears from Jesus is, "When you grow old, you will stretch out your hands, and someone else will . . . take you where you do not wish to go" (John 21:18).

My garden is a wild place. It has its moments of shining glory, mostly the first two weeks of April, before it heads into a slow decline. (That's a function of my tendency to be a strong starter and a slow finisher.) At the high point of my spring I am dutifully pinching off the numerous little buds of the peonies so that the numerous heavy blossoms don't break the branch.

"Every branch in me that doesn't bear fruit, the Father removes, cuts away; and every branch that does bear fruit, he prunes, so that it may bear more fruit" (John 15:2). Either way, you get the knife.

I don't prune my peonies to punish them. I prune them so the fruit—in this case the remaining blossoms—can be bigger and more lush than ever. The peony can channel its power more effectively this way. But other times I prune to help shape the plant when it's been broken by the wind or wounded by insects or burned by the sun. I prune it to help it heal. It's only been recently that I've started to see God's pruning in my life as healing rather than punishment.

"As the Father has loved me, so I love you; abide in my love."

Abiding is an opportunity to trust yourself to the God whose power is flowing like a river; it's a chance to trust yourself to the Gardener who is ready to tend to you and care for you—loving you more than you could imagine. It's to trust in the power of the vine, not in your own efforts, and to live in the knowledge that all the branches on the vine are important. We all bear fruit together.

So what does God want *from* me? The answer begins with recognizing what God wants *for* me.

God wants our trust that the same power that brought forth all that is, is now working on our behalf. To believe that the goodness behind the shattering beauty of the sunset and the fragile vulnerability of the butterflies is the same goodness that seeks our welfare. And that goodness has a face and a name; that goodness has a voice and a message to seek and to save those of us who are lost and looking for home. That Jesus, the Son of God, has come to a humanity who has so forgotten our identity and our purpose that we have lost our collective memory of what it's like to stand up and see the sky.

To trust in the power Jesus knew and lived. To know it would mean everything must change. To change our minds about most of what we know. To be willing to fall back into the water, and let that One carry us to wherever we land. To trust that the riverbanks we hit, the landscapes we see and the rocks we touch are holy—just as we ourselves are. To remind ourselves that we live surrounded by Love.

Over time we could get used to that. We might even start abiding in it.

Childlike Trust

"Never grow up! Always grow down!"

This was the advice of the eccentric, creepy grandma in Roald Dahl's fantasy childhood book *George's Marvelous Medicine*.[1] George succeeds in touching the edges of an invisible world by concocting a potion that causes his grandmother to grow through the roof before becoming so small she disappears from sight.

As with all of Dahl's books the climax takes place largely within young George as he experiences the stunning power to change his situation. He is eight years old and gets a sense of just how wonderful, how fantastic, *how magical*, he really is.

Dahl traded in children's fantasies. He never forgot that sense of wonder, of amazement and fascination they traffic in. Reading Dahl at night as I tucked my kids into bed would mean erupting into hysterics as my kids heard their own dreams brought to life in these characters.

I think Jesus would have loved Roald Dahl. In fact, I know he would have. When most respectable men had little to say to or about children, Jesus often found himself surrounded by them. And not just because their parents had dragged them to "church" but because there was an attraction, a fantasy-inducing magnetism about Jesus that children, especially, could relate to. The words of Jesus took them into other worlds. Jesus' words excited their imaginations and inspired them to ask, *What if?*

Jesus refused to believe this is a grownups-only world. In practice or in his imagination.

One day, his disciples tried to stop a bunch of parents from bringing their kids around. They had the audacity to bring "even their infants," as the Gospel writer Luke writes in his record. The disciples sounded exasperated. But Jesus called them over and said, "Let the little children come to me, . . . for it is to such as these that the kingdom of heaven belongs" (see Matthew 19). Okay, kind of crazy to adult ears. But then, Jesus goes one better, saying in another place, "Unless *you* become like children, you will never enter the kingdom of heaven" (Matthew 18:3).

More than just welcoming children, Jesus says they are the examples for all of us older, supposedly wiser grownups!

So what is it about children that we adults have forgotten? And how does it relate to moving us from our defended positions into something that looks like life?

Confidence

A while back I was in my local grocery store when I found myself in the vegetable aisle hearing a young voice pretending to be gruff, "Okay lady, put 'em up!" Since I was ripping the corn silk back in a furtive effort to see how good it was, I briefly thought I'd been busted by the produce manager. Until I turned around to see a six-year-old cowboy dressed from his Rodeo Bill hat right down to his brown Denver boots. His plastic-handled guns were drawn. I could tell by his badge that he was a sheriff.

Did I mention I live in downtown Chicago?

I slowly put down the corn and raised my hands as the cowboy sheriff nodded and carefully warned me, "Don't let it happen again" before darting off to find his mother.

This is the world of childhood. And these are its inhabitants: Little people who at any point can confidently and eagerly become whoever they want to be. It's playful to be sure. And imaginative and creative, but underneath it all there is an essential confidence, a security that healthy children occupy.

I think this essential confidence is something we can easily lose as we grow up. We lose that fundamental belief that we are okay. Actually, more than okay, that we are great. And when we lose that sense within ourselves, then we begin the lifelong preoccupation with finding validation from outside of ourselves. We don't get it from inside—so we look for it outside.

Not all of this is bad, of course. As we grow toward maturity, it's necessary to do some realistic self-assessment. But sometimes we do it in ways that on the surface are just kind of, well, pitiful.

Like the motherhood award that I received almost fifteen years ago.

To put it in context, I was a young mother who realized that this path of parenting was a path of coming to terms with my inadequacy. This is the way of mothers, isn't it? You realize you will never love these precious little ones in the way they deserve to be loved. You will never have enough wisdom for the decisions at hand. You will never be patient enough to face the challenges of the day. As I look back over my years of mothering, I wince when I think of some of the screams, the threats, the four-letter words that I occasionally hurled. I've busted toys that inexplicably went off in the middle of the night and, at least in one moment, hurled a PlayStation out the window.

This is the part of motherhood they never tell you about: You'll never be smart enough to help with calculus or maybe even the everyday math books of elementary school. And many, many nights you'll go to bed wishing you had acted better, loved better, known better.

Maybe that's why, early on, I made up this story—this absurd falsehood that my kids believed. *For years.*

Sumner (my oldest) was probably about six when I announced, "Yes, *I do know* what I'm talking about. I have won the 'Mother of the Year' award." I gave him the details on it: I had competed against mothers all around the world. The final was held in Cape Town, South Africa, where I proudly received the grand prize. Sumner would periodically ask me why he couldn't remember this ceremony, *Had I left him at home?*

I was sorry he couldn't remember this, but it was true.

I trotted out that Mother of the Year award whenever my authority was questioned. Or when I was getting some pushback. Not only did Sumner believe it for a long time, he even used it as a weapon against his younger brother and sister as they came on the scene. We'd be driving around, and the little ones in the back would give me some flak about the radio station or my opinions on summer camps, and Sumner would twist around from his exalted position in the front and say, "She won the Mom of the Year award, dummy!"

Why yes, I smiled. Yes, *I had.*

I kept up this silly charade, off and on, for years. When Sumner got into junior high we had so many more pressing concerns that my amazing Mother Award kind of slipped off my radar screen. That is, until the afternoon my second son, Porter, came home from second grade, dragging his book bag behind him. With a sad-puppy look on his face, Porter stood in the kitchen and sadly announced, "There *is no* Mother of the Year award." He had bragged on his mother to his friends, and they had set him straight.

Yes. I still feel bad about that—even as I write it down years later. I know counseling sorts would have a field day with this incident. What compelled me to create such a ridiculous story? The Mother of the Year award started as an imaginative fantasy. All of our imaginations ran amok during that window of time. And in general I think I was just playing around, like we did about most things when we had small children in the house. It was a time when our collective creativities were blessedly out of control. From reenacting the feeding of the five thousand, or the busy library system frequented by the stuffed animals, to performing elaborate funeral services for the demise of a pet turtle, our family teetered on the edge of actuality.

But in retrospect, at a deeper level, I think what I was craving was some validation—some certainty—that while I wasn't the best mother, I was good enough. I needed that external validation that it was going to be all right, that perhaps a little bit because of me and likely a lot in spite of me, these little people I loved more than anything in the world were going to turn out just fine.

I wanted to recover from some place *outside* of me what the produce department cowboy sheriff knew *inside* himself instinctively. I wanted to have that essential confidence restored. And this time with higher stakes. What I really needed, I realize now, was some sense of trust in the fullness of the story. A trust that somehow I was sufficient enough for what I was called to do.

I could never see beyond the stage I was in at the moment, and I kept getting stuck in stage after stage: the exhaustion of infancy, the power struggles of preschool, the irritations of junior high, the rapid-fire mood shifts of teenagers.

That's a feeling mothers—parents—know. Of course. But it's the story of all of us, isn't it? That's what we all experience. That's the story of our lives. As we hurtle from one crisis stage to another, we crave some sign that it's going to be all right. If we could only be confident in that, then we can meet what's ahead. Whether it's right up there around the bend in the road or in the vegetable aisle.

My kids were confident because they were ultimately confident in me. Regardless of whether I had won an award or not. Their confidence in me made them confident in themselves. We were interconnected. Jesus saw something similar, I think. Jesus trusted in the fullness of God and the unfolding story of life that encompassed every person together. He knew and lived the confidence of what the apostle Paul was going to describe several decades later when Paul wrote, quoting a Greek poet, "In [God], we live and move and have our being" (Acts 17:28). Jesus trusted this essential goodness—this love—of the One he knew as his Father through every circumstance and challenge. That's what Jesus is offering us as well.

Paula, a teacher friend of mine, gave me a great insight into what Jesus is offering. In the elementary grades, she said, when kids are asked the question "Who in here is an artist?" half the hands shoot up. By sixth grade you ask the same question, and maybe one or two hands go up. All the others—the other artists and cowboys and makers of magical potions—hadn't been externally validated for the creative gifts that were in them, so they had self-selected out. Slowly that part of them that said, *You can create and imagine and dream,* slowly that part had been buried.[2]

Become like a child again.

Spontaneity

Not only do children tend to assert a sense of confidence in their own possibilities, children also exhibit a peculiar ability to fully engage in the moment at hand. We adults seem to lose that. As grownups we regularly urge each other to *live in the present* or *be in the moment.* Just the fact that we have to instruct each other in that direction is a clue to how far off we've wandered. You say that to a kid, and they'll just stare at you like you've lost your mind. Children have an instinctive way of feeling everything acutely in the moment while it's happening.

Throughout high school my son Sumner spent the summer working full time as a camp counselor. His charges were five-year-old to nine-year-old campers. One night over dinner he was going through how most of his day is spent. "I fill out at least twenty accident reports a day!" he vented.

"Every single thing that happens to one of these kids is such a big deal!" he said. "Every time they fall down, I have to look at their knees or their elbows—even if I can't see anything there. If they bump into each other, they will cry until I examine their heads to tell them there is nothing there! Everything they feel is intense and immediate."

Hmm. Yes. That's it exactly, I thought.

Because, of course, that's the way kids are! Every joy, every grief is *the event* that is happening right that moment.

In joyful things especially there is no reason to move from that moment too quickly. How many times have you thrown a kid into a swimming pool, and they pop back up screaming and laughing, and the first thing they say is "Do it again!" You lift them back up, throw them in again, farther out this time so they use up some extra seconds of swim time. Then they eagerly get back to the side and the first thing is "Do it again!"

Many great saints have talked about this childlike quality of joy that emanates from our Creator God.

Tony Campolo, talking about the childlike heart of God, speculated as to how God created daisies:

Did he just say, "Daisies, be!"? Or after he created the first little daisy, did something childlike in the heart of God yell, "Do it again!"? So God created daisy number two. And once more, something inside of God said, "Do it again!" And daisy number three was created. And then four, five, and six. And each time, God clapped his hands and shouted, "Do it again! Do it again! Do it again!" And fifty billion trillion daisies later, the great God of the universe is still jumping up and down, clapping his hands, and yelling, "Do it again! Do it again!"[3]

I don't know about you, but I get tired just thinking about being thrown back into the pool over and over and over again. I'm often racing ahead to the next moment or anxiously waiting on the present moment to end; that is, of course, when I'm not reliving a moment in the past. I'm often everywhere *except* in the present moment.

But it's the present moment where God actually is, and Jesus knew this. Children live with all the energy and passion they have at hand in the moment at hand. But as Jesus pointed out, and as our lives well demonstrate, we are often so anxious about the future (*What are we going to wear? What are we going to eat?*) or so remorseful over the past, that we have a hard time simply being in the moment *that is.*

A Sense of Self

People who are worried about their self-image, their worth, their value usually cannot go on with life without being overly concerned about themselves.

One night a family was awakened to a terrific thunderstorm. It was one of those thunder-roaring, lightning-flashing, windows rattling variety of a storm. When the father woke up, he ran upstairs to his daughter's bedroom, imagining he would find his preschooler frightened and quivering under the covers. Instead, when he got to her room, the little girl was standing on the windowsill, leaning spread-eagle against the glass, with all this lightning and thunder going on right outside.

"I think God is trying to take my picture," she said, when her dad entered the room.[4]

I think God is trying to take my picture! Wow. That's knowing something about your own importance—about how God values you. When was the last time you imagined God wanting to take your picture? For some of us it's been a while, hasn't it? We're so down on ourselves and what we haven't done, or what we've done poorly. Or equally painful, we're so riddled with guilt about the things we've done that are never to be undone, that we can't imagine God in any state other than exasperation.

That's one of the reasons Jesus came.

Jesus came into the world to do something to you that would enable you to feel differently about yourself. Something that would enable you to experience life and experience God differently. Of course, there's a lot wrong with you. Just ask your spouse or your close friends. There's a lot wrong with me too. These are some of the things we learn as we grow up. But they are not the whole story. "Jesus Himself comes into the world not only to die for our sins but to come into your life and to absorb from you everything that is dirty and ugly and negative and make you His own—to free you from all of that."[5]

We need to know something about our own value. We need to know our own place that is recovered in and by and through the love of Jesus. We need to be released from our self-fixation because we are finally so sufficiently assured of our worth that we can live an open life. We can be open. Open to God and open to other people. That's the good news of Jesus. And that's something of what Jesus saw when he took that little boy in front of the crowd of men and said, "Unless you become like a little child, you will never enter the kingdom of God."

One of the most loved and admired miracles recorded in the Bible starts with just such a child. One afternoon, on a hot hill close to the Galilean Sea a multitude of more than five thousand people gathered to hear Jesus teach. After a while they got hungry. With hunger comes restlessness, irritation and impatience. The disciples were picking up on the changing mood in the crowd. Nervous themselves, they asked Jesus to send the people home. *This is getting out of hand!* I imagine them thinking to themselves.

It was at that moment that a little boy stepped forward—a young boy, confident that he had something of importance, something worth sharing. Admittedly, it wasn't much. You might have laughed if you had been there to look at the basket the boy solemnly held out. It was just five fish and seven loaves of bread. Imagine the confidence to even bring such a thing forward at such a moment of high drama. If it had been anybody but a kid, you might have thought he was mocking you, making light of the very real needs of the people.

Jesus pronounced it perfect. And with those small gifts offered confidently and without apology or shame, Jesus used it to feed the thousands on the mountainside. We call it a miracle. But it was a miracle that began with one anonymous child having a sense of just how important he really was (see John 6:1-13).

Become like a little child.

A Sense of Family

Ancient texts tell stories about the early Christians who left society beginning in the early fourth century, retreating to the deserts to follow God. Called "desert fathers and mothers," they believed the best way they could follow God was by moving deep into the unrelenting heat of the deserts of Egypt. Further and further south they pushed along the uninhabited tracks of land along the lower Nile River. Their desire for holy solitude led them to build mud huts where they could live and practice devotion to God in undisturbed and uninterrupted seclusion.

Archaeologists know that the homes—initially far apart from each other—began to move closer and closer together. The monks explained it by asking the question, "Whose feet were we to wash when we were alone?"

Likely you see what they were getting at: We can't really be followers of God all by ourselves. There is another element—a horizontal element—that must be present if we are going to become the people we were meant to be.

I once attended an interfaith dialogue led by a local Muslim cleric who opened his talk by noting that the idea of the Trinity—the Father, Son and Holy Spirit—was one of the most scandalous doctrines of Christianity to him.

"How could the power of the all-powerful God be shared between any others?" he wondered. The idea of shared or distributed power was simply anathema to a monotheist who viewed the very essence of Allah to be that of a single, supreme, autonomous deity. God rules alone, he intoned.

I've thought about his speech several times since. I don't know enough about Islam to know if this image of God ruling alone, aloof, self-contained and impregnable is the primary expression of God's nature in Islam. But I do know that the premise that particular cleric was getting at is fundamentally different from the Christian concept.

The Christian faith says we have a God who shares, a God who is self-giving, a God whose very essence is located in relationship and community. I realize most of us don't spend a lot of time thinking about the Christian doctrine of the Trinity. The doctrine says that the three persons of the Godhead exist in a mutually dependent, creative, life-giving expression. At the core of that relationship is an unshakable bond of love.

Everything that is, is an expression of that community: the oneness of the creation itself, the intertwined nature of personhood and our innate desire to be in relationships with others.

The first book of the Bible, Genesis, means "beginnings." That book elaborates on the theme that people are created in the image of God. There is a "God mark," you might say, emblazoned on us. We are reflections of God, and the nobility and grace of humanity reflect God's likeness. We create and nurture and love as reflections of our Creator who creates and nurtures and loves.

Yet I wonder if "God's image," "God's likeness," is telling us something about not only what it means to be an individual human being but also what it means to be part of humankind—the community of humanity. Surely the nature of love and interdependence that exists in a *triune* God marks our nature, meant for love and interdependence in relationships among ourselves.

I'm not trying to be trite about something so important, but I believe there is a relationship within humanity that the Trinity points to, and we have ignored it to our peril. Apart from one another, we remain undone. We find our completeness together, in connection.

We *are* family—part of the large family of God that must be recovered if we're really going to live in the big community of God. You and I are created to live out God's intentions by living in authentic interdependent relationships with others.

This interdependence is another thing Jesus was asking us to recover when he urged us to become like a little child again. Children have a breathtaking capacity for seeing their similarities, not their differences. Our church has operated a preschool for years that is a mirror of the Chicago landscape. Wealthy diplomats' kids from Japan, Turkey and Canada have spent years playing alongside kids from the roughest housing projects in Chicago. To wander through the hallways is to travel down the halls of the United Nations where names like Muhammad, Hiroyu, Maximilian, Deshawn and Itzhak are written in big block letters above their lockers, lined with pictures of kids of all skin colors reading, playing and singing together.

Kids have an innate sense of the big family. They are just happy to be part of it. And the bigger the family is, the better.

Jesus saw this oneness. It comes out in different ways throughout his teaching. "I have sheep who do not belong to this fold," Jesus says to a group of Jewish men who knew something about the ways of sheep herding. "They will listen to my voice. So there will be one flock, one shepherd" (John 10:16). Jesus kept expanding his focus to the world. "I have come to *the world*, that they might have life," he said.

Yet for his followers—me and perhaps you too—we have narrowed his message until it seems to be for a selective group of people. And they just happen to be people that look just like me, think just like me and aspire to the same things I aspire to.

The fullness of Jesus' message is expressed—the expansiveness of God's family is expressed—in the solidarity of people who realize the common bond between them is an interdependent love. (Just like the Trinity.)

Emmanuel Katongole, former codirector of the Center for Reconciliation at Duke University, tells a powerful story about what this can look like. It was the Easter season of 1994 when the majority Tutsi Christians tried to eliminate their Hutu's brothers and sisters in a terrible genocide that blanketed the country of Rwanda. Even after the bloodshed stopped six months later, roving bands of militia and racist thugs continued to roam the streets of that bloody country.

On March 18, 1997, three years after the genocide, militia attacked the secondary school at Nyange in Rwanda. The students had finished supper and their evening prayer, and they were in the classrooms doing their daily prep. The rebels attacked Senior 4 and Senior 5 classes and commanded the students to separate into two groups: Tutsi and Hutu. The students, who were fifteen and sixteen years old, refused. We are all Rwandans, they replied. The rebels then shot at them indiscriminately and threw grenades into the classroom. Thirteen students were killed in all.

All because they stood up in their differences and said, *We stand together.*

Most of us would quake at the idea of emulating this example. But this example isn't about where it starts. This example is about the kind of love that emerges out of the daily practice of solidarity with our brothers and sisters. We start with simply standing alongside others. With our neighbor and with those across town. With those who think and pray in a different manner from us. We acknowledge that there are ties between us, and those ties make us family with each other.

When Jesus said become like a little child again, he was offering us a way to recover something we've forgotten in all of our growing up. He was offering us a way to "grow down" in the words of Roald Dahl. A way of remembering something that's been lost to many of us. Confidence, spontaneity, a sense of self and a sense of connectedness. I experienced all of that in a powerful encounter I had with a quiet and determined man outside his tin home among the shacks of Managua, Nicaragua.

I was with a group from Opportunity International, a microlending group that offers very small loans (as low as $50) to the "poorest of the poor" in order to spur economic independence that transforms communities. People who receive loans meet together to hold themselves accountable and make decisions about how to further invest in one another. The system is called a "Trust Bank." We had come to see for ourselves what such a modest loan could do to lift ambitious people out of poverty.

The days had been packed solid, and on our final day in Nicaragua it was just after lunch when our little van stopped at the home of Juan Perez. Juan had received his first loan from Opportunity International almost three years before. We exited the van and the heat of the day was suddenly matched by the heat coming out of Juan's house. The five of us, already sweating, walked slowly to the open doorway of a concrete block structure, about forty square feet in size. Walking in, I looked around and saw a big open room with some rudimentary furniture. A tin roof covered the room, and it began about a foot above where the blocked walls stopped.

And all I could smell and all I could see—on the floor and on the makeshift table—was bread. Pan after pan of freshly baked bread sitting on top of the dirt floor, stacked on the one table. Juan had built an oven out of cinder blocks in the corner of his home and rigged up a bare light bulb in it. Looking in, I saw another ten pans or so of bread in the oven.

The field guide we were traveling with had a few stock questions she had asked every loan recipient we'd met. "How long ago did you receive your first loan? How has life changed for your children?" Those sorts of questions.

We listened politely as Juan gave responses we had heard from other such families. Then I asked, through the translator, "How many days of the week do you work, Juan?" He paused and then said with his eyes down, like he was thinking it through, "I work every day of the week. I have worked every day since my first loan, every day for the last three years. If I don't bake bread, my customers could find someone else to buy it from. So I have it for them every day."

Juan paused. Then he looked up and said proudly, "You see, before I met my loan officer, I had nothing. No. I had less than nothing. And now, now, look at all I have."

Juan Perez, standing there barefoot, in tattered shorts, no shirt, with his pregnant wife next to him, knew he was a man at the top of his world. He knew who he was. He knew something of his own value. He knew something about what the trust bank had done for him and what he was now capable of doing for others.

A little boy on a mountainside knew the same thing.

"Unless you become as a little child, you will not see the kingdom of heaven," Jesus said.

The unshakable confidence for the future, a deep sense of joy, spontaneous and free that comes from knowing your value and your worth. This is the gospel of Jesus Christ—the gospel that makes people fully alive, that makes us into little children. The gospel that recovers the spontaneous joy of an earlier time.

The gospel that makes us believe in the future.

It's the gospel that empowers Juan Perez to know he is somebody and makes a little boy believe he has something to share.

Become like a little child.

Part Three

Finding Real Connection

Restoring Your Identity

I was standing at the checkout at the uber-hip Urban Outfitters (obviously buying something for my kids), virtually turning my purse upside down while I looked in all the pockets for my credit card. I was starting to get a little unnerved and trying to remember where I had last used that card, when "Randy," the thin, multipierced, multitattooed clerk outfitted in a black polyester golf shirt from the 1970s soothingly—breathlessly—crooned, "It's all good."

I looked up at him, holding my credit card in triumph, and replied without thinking, "God said the very same thing!"

Randy's cool vibe changed instantly. His eyes widened and his lips pursed into the shape of a little "o" as he got that "religious fanatic warning" look on his face. I had to assure him, God didn't tell me that over breakfast this morning. But, I assured Randy, whether he knew it or not, he was quoting God. It's good, God says. *It's all good.* It was unclear to me whether Randy was comforted by this.

God says, *It's all good* seven times in the first chapter of the first book of the Bible. God, seemingly thrilled with this project of creation, says, "It is good."

And on top of that, there is one thing that is *very good*. There is one especially good aspect of creation brought out of the chaos that God speaks to and enters into relationship with. There is one created being that isn't formed "after its kind" as the writer of Genesis describes much of creation. This one is formed after God alone.

One creature whom God chooses to carry the spark of God's own self. "Let us make man in our image, after our likeness," it says in Genesis 1:26 (KJV). (Don't get hung up on the "man" part. It's a Hebrew word, ʾādām, that the ancient scribes used. Scholars think the term refers more to the complexion of humans since the word is also used for "ground" or "soil" in other places.)

Humans will be told later to not create any graven images of God. But this same God did allow one created item to bear his image: You.

Somehow, in some way, we show something about the nature of God.

At our core there is something particularly and especially wonderful and true about us as humans. We have intrinsic value that none of our paltry actions can completely erase; we have a dignity that cannot be taken away, a worth that is never removed. We are the image of God, and God is known in some way by creatures who live in the realm of free history, where power is received, decisions are made and commitments are honored.

And not only is our nature marked by God, but the implication that we are these small image-bearers of God in the world—where we work and play and study—means that God has chosen to govern, to act in the world, not by some sort of autocratic fiat but by men and women—you and me. We have the freedom to exercise authority, to make choices, to mirror the Creator's artistry and activity.

And this can't be taken away. Our glorious vision and creativity can be narrowed, reduced and twisted, but it cannot be eliminated. It's just not possible. We receive it at birth. All of us do.

The End of Emptiness

The challenge for real connection the reality that our sense of our intrinsic worth has been beaten down, denied or ignored for so long that we've lost touch with it. Jesus came to restore our identities—he came to give us our lives back! But not the old lives we've become used to. He came to give back the original life—the life before it became tattered and ragged. He gives a life where you know you are blessed and desired. A life where you know you are loved.

It was over a salad lunch in a crowded downtown cafeteria when I first had a long conversation with Nancy. An attractive woman in her forties, she had been attending our church for a little more than a year. She volunteered at church and quickly established a reputation for her kindness and compassion. This was in addition to a demanding job working in the Loop in downtown Chicago.

As soon as we sat down, however, a fuller reality about Nancy began to emerge. The Nancy who, from about eight years old, lay in bed night after night, hoping her father wasn't going to come into her room and begin fondling her. The Nancy who tried to tell her mother what was going on only to be dismissed and discounted. The Nancy who internalized the abuse of both her mother and her father by believing that perhaps this is what she deserved. This is the Nancy who has gone through one abusive marriage and was struggling to put another abusive relationship behind her.

This was the Nancy who was prepared to do anything to believe a different message about herself. She just didn't know how to believe it. How to even begin to imagine a different message than the one she had been told for so long.

To hear she had dignity and worth? Value and significance? Those had just been words to her. Words without any power or influence until she walked into the doors of our church one Sunday and heard me tell a story about a very small, very old, saintly lady named Lois, whom we were honoring on that day.

In worship that particular morning I had told the congregation about a recent incident. Lois, a senior citizen, had worked all morning at our meal program: chopping vegetables, cooking and serving lunch. After volunteering several hours, she asked if one of our staff members could give her a ride to her doctor's office about twenty blocks away, so I volunteered. As we drove south through downtown Chicago, Lois asked me to let her off at an intersection rather than the address of her doctor's office. Lois was adamant, no matter how strongly I pressed for the address, she kept saying she just wanted to get out at this particular intersection. Finally, Lois admitted to me she wanted to be dropped off at this particular spot so she could find the homeless guy that regularly stood there. "Today is his birthday, and I got him a card with a few goodies."

"When I heard that story of Lois, I just lost it," Nancy said. "Hearing how determined Lois was to show this random homeless guy how valued and respected he was made me see for the first time that God is even more determined to find me. And love me too."

I walked away from that lunch once again humbled by the astounding truth that God has given us the opportunity to help each other relearn his essential message that *we are all good*.

There is a letter near the end of the New Testament that most people don't read very frequently. It's a letter attributed to Peter, one of the disciples who had plenty of incidents and actions he likely wanted to forget.

This letter, simply called "The First Letter of Peter," was written to an audience scattered all around southern Italy, the Greek peninsula and modern-day Turkey. "To God's elect" the letter begins, "strangers in the world, scattered throughout Pontus, Galatia, Cappadocia, Asia and Bithynia" (NIV 1984). This was a group that had very little in common with each other except they were all outsiders.

They were people without voting rights or even landholding privi-leges. People with limited legal protections.

They were considered second-tier in the Roman Empire—sharing an echo of the same message: *You're not worth very much around here.* Peter wrote to remind them of a different message and a different ritual. "You have been born anew," he said. *You have a new name: you are holy people.* That identity as holy people should mark them in the way the image of God marked them from the very beginning.

That's your name, Peter said. Now live into it.

Oh, if it were only that easy! I can almost hear you protesting. If only it were that easy for Nancy to put behind her the old scripts, the old names. But those old recordings take a long time to fade.

Even the smallest of slurs can take a long time to get over. My husband's job took us for a few years to Tokyo. A wonderful experience with wonderful people. But you really want to experience what it means to be an outsider, try visiting the homogeneous society of Japan. The experience of standing at the large intersections in Shibuya station in Tokyo—with literally millions of people rushing around me, all of them dark-haired, dark-eyed and darkly dressed—is still so present. Our tall, white family with our brown, blond and red hair stood sorely out of place.

We and all other foreigners were called *Gaijin*. This was a name I heard repeatedly. In the shops while I fumbled for the right change, in the parks when I let the kids run around more freely than appro-priate. Mothers would nod to each other, and in a flurry of Japanese say at least once the word that I knew referred to me: *Gaijin*.

The Tokyo sidewalks were often lined with people giving out mar-keting products—similar to the Magnificent Mile in Chicago, where you have flyers thrust at you for everything from liquidation sales to hair loss treatments. But in Tokyo they sweetened the deal by handing out those flyers along with some pretty useful stuff. Kleenex packages, especially, were a common favorite. The first time I saw this, I thought, *Cool!* I really need some Kleenex! As I approached the man I held out my hand to receive the tissues he was forcing on others. Except as I approached, he pulled his hand away muttering, *Debuchi. Nihonjin desu.* ("I'm sorry. Japanese only.")

It sounds like such a trivial exchange doesn't it? But even now, years later, I can recall my confusion, my shame. I glanced around hurriedly to see if anyone had seen me stupidly reach for the Kleenex. I remember the flash of anger and the simple unfairness of it.

And of course that silly encounter is nothing—utterly insignificant—next to the marks of racism, discrimination and hate experienced by many people I know. How does someone escape the ugly encounter?

How does a son get past the names his drunken father used to call him?

How does a junior high girl get past the nasty things written on the anonymous note? Or, as I sat across the table from Nancy that day, I asked the question this way, "How do you recover from the atrocities done to you by the people who should have loved you best?"

It's the same question you have to ask of Jesus' friend Peter too. How does he move beyond the labels he was given? "Coward." "He who denied." It was the blustery Peter who told Jesus, "I will never betray you! I will never let you down, my friend!" Yet within a few hours of Jesus' arrest Peter had denounced his friend. And it wasn't because he caved under torture-like pressure from an CIA operative. Peter buckled the second some gossiping bystanders turned to him, thought he looked familiar and offhandedly asked. Peter didn't go to the mat for his friend Jesus; he didn't even get in the ring!

Peter needed to have his own identity restored. Perhaps even more than those to whom he was writing, Peter needed to hear that it was possible to begin again—to hear that his identity could be restored. "You are a holy people," he said. "Go and live like it."

Do Over

There is a system of reading and preaching through the Bible in a three-year cycle. This cycle is called "the lectionary." There's not one lectionary but several. The Roman Catholic Church uses one just for them; then there's one that the Anglicans/Episcopalians use; and then there's one called the "common lectionary," which is pretty much what all other Protestants use if they are going to follow a formal program.

There are really only slight differences among them. No matter which lectionary or Scripture cycle you might come upon, stories about John the Baptist come up in the teaching just a few weeks before Christmas. There is no avoiding this locust-eating, bear-hide-wearing prophet. If I could have figured out a way to avoid him, I might have. I used to cringe when his story came up. *Dear Lord,* I'd think, *we're just a few weeks from the baby Jesus!* I would begin my sermon preparation by looking up at the glittered cards of Christmas hope and peace only to look down and find strange John. With the Bethlehem stable practically in our sights I would get up on Sunday morning to deliver the good news from texts with John snarling, "You brood of vipers! Who warned you to flee from the wrath to come?" (Matthew 3:7).

Ouch.

How does all this talk of terror and haste and chopping and fiery flames prepare us for the arrival of the Prince of Peace? What does John's message have to do with a fresh start?

You and I want the warm fuzzies at the end—the stirring in our chest that inspires and uplifts us. But here is the tension: In order to welcome the arrival of Jesus, in order for us to even desire the good news of a fresh start, we have to be able to see what's wrong with the start we are on.

John is preaching that there is a new day coming! "The kingdom of God is at hand!" Jesus is at hand. But to receive Jesus, the people had to come to the realization that something was wrong. That somewhere along the way they had gotten stuck. In order to welcome the kingdom of God into their lives, they had to recognize that there is something wrong that they just couldn't fix without God.

And the same is true for us.

There is another force always threatening to take us under. It seems to hold us captive. We make these bold, courageous *I'm going to do that!* kind of statements. And then in the next hour our resolve is broken, our promises in a heap, our courage gone. Or we say with full conviction, *I will never do that!* and days later, there we are, doing precisely the thing we disavowed. We spin round and round like the wheels of a truck caught in the mud. "I do not understand my own actions," writes Paul in his letter to the church in Rome. "For I do not do what I want, but I do the very thing I hate" (Romans 7:15).

For the apostle Peter as much as for Paul and John the Baptist—and you and me, as well—we have to recognize the *metanoia*—the "changing our mind" process that must happen with every fresh start. To really get the meaning of *metanoia* just think of a time when you missed a turn and found yourself lost. There's that little window of time when you're kind of aware that you might be wrong, and you begin to consider whether you should turn around. You do this little cost-benefit analysis in your head and keep going a little farther just to be sure. Then finally, you're ready to turn around. That moment when you give up on your road and turn around—that's *metanoia*.

The challenge of living into the fresh start is formidable. A few years ago I traveled to Africa with World Vision, a Christian humanitarian agency. Our trip was in November—a perfect month to really decide that this Christmas we were going to do things differently! No more philistine consumerism for us! I returned home determined that all of our family Christmas gifts were going to be donations of cows and goats, bees and buffalos—all given to others. But within weeks I was circling Macy's sale advertisements. It turns out I had a hard time striking the familiar Christmas-spirit chord by buying a goat. I couldn't get this new kind of Christmas to feel like a "fulfilling" experience. It was going to take some practice.

It's on the everyday trivialities that *metanoia* requires the most practice.

John the Baptist talked about the preparation for this fresh start being something like God removing trees from your life. *The trees must fall!* John thunders. Otherwise how will the fresh shoot spring up? Trees must fall in order for the new trees to be planted. The old trees must fall in order for the sun to reach the forest floor, in order for the new green pastures to emerge. These will be pastures that will hold former enemies and overcome old divisions. Or, as Isaiah, an earlier prophet, wrote, they will be pastures where "the wolf and the lamb shall feed together" (see Isaiah 11:1-9; 65:17-25).

It doesn't sound like a Christmas song, but there's no avoiding it. Trees must fall, John affirms. And they must fall now.

What trees must fall in your life? John the Baptist is addressing the religious leaders, the Pharisees and the Sadducees. Their own religious demands and expectations had gotten in the way of seeing the new life that was coming forward. Their religious trees blocked their view of the kingdom of God drawing near to them.

For the prophet Isaiah any tree that stood in the way of peace was a tree that needed to come down. Any tree had to come down if it hindered the establishment of the kingdom of peace, if it prevented people from acting like people who live in the kingdom of peace.

For Peter, it was the tree of his own actions. The tree he had clung to, created by his own power and resolve. The tree that said, *I won't fail!* For Nancy it is the tree of degradation, planted and watered by someone else, that must fall to the ground. Some things have to come down before, finally, the full radiance of the sun can shine.

No matter what trees have to come down, the process by which they come down is a mixture of being both receptive to God's work in your life and then rising to meet that work. Jesus talked about new beginnings in a consistent way. The power of God initiated new beginnings, and people met and acted upon God's initial action. It is decidedly not by our own will power. But it's also true that after a new beginning is offered, there are ways we take hold of it by our actions. It always goes back to the dignity and power God bestows in the creation of humanity.

John Steinbeck describes it as "the glory of the choice!"[1] And it is, definitely, a glorious choice. But it's one that each of us has to make our own.

So what does Jesus do? Jesus sets it in motion. By revealing to us the very face of God, Jesus makes it possible for us to believe that the same God who created and loved us in those opening chapters of the Bible, calling us *very good*—that same God says the same thing now. We are very good.

We are also, Jesus says, very sick. Corporately, we have been caught in systems of violence, pride and domination. Those are systems you and I have created and benefit from. We have not only allowed those trees to grow, we have fertilized and watered them. We have used others and cursed them for using us; we have done outrageous evil and have refused to forgive those who have done evil to us. We have wallowed in self-absorption and personal ambition and called it good and healthy. In all ways we have hoarded the glory given to us and to this planet. We have trampled on it as if all of this around us—creation, those we love and those who love us—were no more than grapes for us to crush into our boozy drinks.

You and I have done this. We call it sin.

But take heart, Jesus said, *my power is greater than the power that did this. And my mercy sews torn things back together. My grace is such that broken pieces are joined together again. And my love—my love is so expansive that there will be no place where it will not find you and bring you home again.*

Born again. For years now that phrase has been associated with a lot of cultural and political baggage. But this is what it means to be born again: You've recognized the trees have to come down. You *want* them to come down. Then when the sun starts to hit your face and you feel the wind at your back, you turn to Jesus—the one with the ax in his hand—and ask him, "Now, what do you want to do in this forest of my life?" After that, you simply cooperate. Day after day after day.

Synthesis

Over time, synthesis starts to emerge. You start to realize that each new beginning, each fresh start is related to the failure, the shortcoming, the defeat that preceded it. You realize there is a deeper, truer story that's being written on (and with) your life. That all of it is connected. As a psalm writer in the middle of the desert said sometime in the eighth century B.C.E., "You have kept count of my tossings; / put my tears in your bottle" (Psalm 56:8). Not one tear is in vain. Nothing is wasted.

It's easy for us to look for all the meaning in one success, all the judgment in one failure, and again that's where we get off course. Because *it's all* connected. The accomplishments we call successes as much as the crashes we call failures. Our moments of courage as well as our moments of cowardice. The times we stepped forward and the times we stayed behind. All of it has meaning and is important to the arc of the big story in ways our dim eyes will not yet see. But our spirits can sense it, and our souls can know it.

This synthesis is radically different from the way most of us think about things. We slice and dice our way through situations, people and problems. We think first in terms of what's good or bad, what's moving us forward, or what's holding us back. It's deceptively easy to imagine decisions as binary choices.

As long as we see our lives as a dichotomy, however, the farther away we stay from the real synthesis that God intends for us. To return to Psalm 23, David recounts the experience of a man who is living in the rich milieu of life—good and bad, secure and frightening. Everything at the same time. And he accepts it all. Understanding his life journey as one lived in the "shadow of the valley of death" while also eating a rich feast in the midst of it, at a table that God has "prepared" for him. The writer knew that all of it was part of the work of God.

Synthesis begins when you understand you have nothing to hide and nothing to gain by denying what is. At the same time, you recognize this deeper, truer story that God is writing is one where nothing is lost.

For a number of years our church community was blessed by a wonderful young couple in their late twenties. They had moved to Chicago after graduating from college. I liked them immediately. Both were engaged in the needs of others and the needs of the world. They brought their faith in Christ to every encounter and situation they experienced, and each of them quickly became leaders in our church community.

Yet it was clear after only a few months in Chicago that one of them was struggling to find his purpose, his fit. While his wife was quickly able to find a great job as soon as she completed her master's degree, the husband seemed stuck. But he was a taciturn Midwesterner and rarely complained—or even let on what was going on beneath the surface.

Several years later Tyson sent me a long email detailing the pain and the glory he had experienced in those Chicago years. As he tells his story, listen for this growing awareness of synthesis:

The entire time Lindsay and I lived in Chicago was tough. I had a degree from a prestigious Christian college and I worked at the Y—as a lifeguard! My friends were accountants, lawyers—they were successful. I followed up on every contact they gave me, put myself out there for every position I heard about—I even worked double shifts at the Y. For months, I worked the early and late shifts, getting six hours of sleep a night, to prove myself. But when a job opened up—a promotion offered—I was the one passed over.

One afternoon, I was in my chair at the pool—guarding—but wishing I would die. I had failed at everything I had put my hand to.

And that's when it happened. I heard a voice. Not audibly, but inside. "I have something more for you."

Over the next few days, I can only describe something as a "growing warmness" starting to take over all that empty pain I had been carrying inside. I started to realize that God wanted me to be at the YMCA and to be a lifeguard. And I started to see all these possibilities, and opportunities I had been missing. They were right under my nose.

I was still getting rejected. It was another year and a half before I got a job. A real job. But in those eighteen months everything had changed. Now I realize I wouldn't take back that experience for anything.[2]

This is the kind of humble, accepting engagement that synthesis can offer us. It's not the kind of acceptance that pretends to "let go and let God" in that bumper-sticker, sound-bite way. It's not the kind of hollow engagement that declares that God is "my copilot." It's acceptance and engagement that lives the mystery of what the early church writer Irenaeus said in the second century, "The glory of God is man fully alive!"[3] This is the cry of a man who has understood that Jesus is serious about redeeming everything. There is nothing that can't be used and won't be used to make that glory visible and compelling in your life.

It's all good.

12

Imagine Love

The word love gets thrown around with the casualness of flinging clothes toward the hamper. All around we are singing, writing and emoting about love, panting for love, people are falling in and out of love. Inside the church we are busy counseling those with raging hormones—painstakingly working through the different types of love (*erōs* or *phileō*) in ways that bemuse, baffle and likely annoy most reasonable people.

I know it's important to nail down descriptions and terminologies. But in my life I know love and its power by experience. My ill-fated first marriage was to a man who became a Christian through my "witness." That is to say, I told him I couldn't continue dating him unless he wanted to take Jesus seriously in the way I did at the time. Soon, Nigel was all in. Nigel's commitment to God led him to seminary—where, with a lot of work and the benefit of our two incomes, he was able to finish in lightning-fast time with no debt—emerging as a minister fully empowered to preach "the good news." Except— after the Bible study classes and the Sunday morning preaching gigs, our life was anything but good news. The love of God we talked so much about was almost completely missing in the way we related and cared for each other.

Perhaps it won't surprise you to know that when my first *very* Christian husband became increasingly mean and my *very* Christian marriage went south, marrying another devout Christian was not high on my list.

That's why, when I first met Terry, I didn't ask him a lot of questions about what he believed. I just knew how he acted and how he interacted with me. I didn't have an orthodoxy checklist of "what truths he named essential," but I did know that he held his own power loosely—not needing to win an argument every time. I saw how his affection for me was surprisingly free from expected outcomes. In the beginning of our relationship I began to dimly realize that this man was going to love me no matter what. I couldn't actually do anything to make me more lovable to him. I could excel and he would celebrate with me; I could fail and he would be a kind voice of encouragement; I could be angry and he would be (generally) understanding.

Terry loved me. Full stop. Period. No buts or howevers. No contingencies or preconditions. Somewhere it hit me: This is how God loves. This is how Jesus loves. God doesn't love us only if we're good. God isn't only proud of us until we fail or patient until suddenly the game's over. God just loves. We change in response to that love. It's as simple as that. The filling, flooding love of Jesus allows us to change. We want to change—we almost can't help but desire to change in the face of this love.

Hard to imagine, you may be thinking. Maybe you feel too far removed from the words of Jesus—from the life of Jesus—to even conceive of what he must have been all about. Maybe it's just been too much time, too much distance between the old Sunday school teacher and where you are now. You may be like the lead character in one of Jesus' favorite stories.

The writer Luke records Jesus telling a little vignette about how important sheep are to the shepherd. Jesus describes a shepherd who tends to many sheep, but one of them wanders off (see Luke 15:1-7).

I was probably twenty-five years old before I ever met an actual shepherd: I mean a guy who made his living tending and sheering sheep. But that wasn't the case in the time and place where the life of Jesus was recorded. Many of Jesus' listeners *were* shepherds. They would have resonated with stories about how vulnerable a sheep could be. On their own, sheep are easy prey, facing all the stronger, faster animals out there. Jesus' audience would have understood that the odds of the shepherd finding a lost sheep before the jackals and wolves did were remote. And they would have understood intuitively that after a few hours of looking, the prudent thing for the shepherd to do is simply give up. To stop looking, call it a day, mourn the loss of that one sheep and return to the business of looking after the rest of the flock.

It must have sounded disorienting, then, to hear Jesus say, "I've come after the one."

I've come after the lost one, the one that most others have given up for dead—the one far away. That's who I am looking for, Jesus says. The one sheep who, either because of its own strength and speed took off ahead of the flock, or because of curiosity wandered down a different trail, or fell behind because of sickness, fatigue or disinterest. It doesn't matter how the sheep was separated. The point is, Jesus says, the Shepherd will never stop looking.

Jesus wasn't just talking about sheep. He was talking about me. He was talking about you. And through a story he was inviting people to see something about how important they were to the God of the universe. Imagine his task: Getting people to understand that the *God of the universe* noticed them. As individuals. Jesus was inviting them to see the lengths God would go to find that one who was alone, out in the world by him- or herself.

So maybe you can relate a little bit to that lost sheep. Maybe you've been hovering along the edges of the crowd—hanging near the back. And now and again you catch Jesus looking at you.

Right now, you think, you have a lot on your mind. These faith questions—well, they're big and sometime when you have time, you'll get around to thinking about them. But right now, maybe you're mulling over the way someone slighted you a couple of weeks ago. Maybe you're caring for an aging mother, and in the quiet of the night you whisper to yourself that it might be better for her to just die. Maybe you're caring for a child and you're wondering if you're really up to this challenge.

You look over at that person sharing your bed and you wonder, *Who are you?* You go to work and you wonder, *What's the point? I went to college for this?* You wonder if you're in the wrong profession; you worry that you'll become an old woman with regrets, an old man with nothing to show for his efforts.

I'm looking for you, Jesus says. *You don't see me, but I see you*, Jesus says. *I hear you whistling in the dark, keeping your fears at bay. I know how your heart races when you think about death.*

But listen to what else I know: You don't have to live standing on the edge, just beyond the circle. I know other things. I've got plans for you. I'm looking for you. To restore you. I want to bring you home. Home to yourself and to me. Home to your purpose. I want to throw you a party.

The Shepherd won't stop looking.

I Am with You

One of the more startling and misunderstood parts of his ministry was his *radical identification* with those who were, in some way or another, lost to the social mainstream. He didn't just reach out; he ventured into the kinds of places where people get lost.

The first public picture we have of Jesus is an event that foreshadows his ministry and future action. It takes place miles outside Jerusalem — and even farther from the town of Nazareth, where Jesus was raised — along the banks of a muddy river (see Matthew 3:1-17).

The Jordan River is located in present-day southern Israel, close to its disputed Jordanian border. It's a waterway running from the Sea of Galilee to the Dead Sea. Today the river is so filthy that portions of it have been closed off altogether. It was likely a dirty place even then. People have long dumped their sewage and waste into rivers, and there is no reason to imagine why this wouldn't have been the case at the time when Jesus first appeared on the public stage.

On the day Jesus came to the Jordan River, the scene in the river ravine would have been pretty typical. There was John the Baptist, an early advocate for living off the grid.

Day after day John and his followers preached a message of apocalyptic warning. Now, growing up, I recall traveling down some of those rural central Florida back roads, and I would see hand-painted signs nailed to scrawny pine trees admonishing folks to "TURN OR BURN!" This was tame next to what John the baptizer spat out.

Everyone was interested. Certainly the religious establishment, the ruling groups were interested in just who this powerful one was going to be. We're told that many from the religious parties known as the Sadducees and the Pharisees watched while people made their way to John. If you were to read this account in Matthew's Gospel, you could well imagine that some of the important people crowding the hillside watching were Roman spies as well. People were listening carefully to John's words, waiting to overhear something seditious — something that could, perhaps, cause him to lose his head.

But among the onlookers was another group — a larger group — making their way to the river. These were the people who did want to turn their lives around. These were people who didn't want to keep living the way they were living.

They were from all walks of life—but with a single common feature. They wanted something better. They were people who had slept with people they weren't supposed to sleep with, and they felt how wrong it was. They were people who had lied to their friends and cheated their business partners because of fear. They were people who had grown small and petty, envying their neighbors and jealous of others' success. They were people who lost their tempers, who spread lies, who had cursed others and struck out in rage.

One after another they went under the water, baptized by John in an act of repentance and contrition. John scarcely paused as the line filed in front of him. Until that day he looked up, reaching for the next body, and stared into the face of Jesus, the one who simply called himself the Son of Man.

What are you doing here, Jesus?

This moment—this first public moment of Jesus' life—is recorded in all four of the Gospel narratives. The writer Matthew captured the bewilderment, the flurry of awkwardness, that permeated the moment. You get the feeling John started to back away, trying to prevent what Jesus is about to do

No, no! This is wrong. Why do you come to me to be baptized? I need to be baptized by you! Why are you in line here, Jesus?

This was the "sinners" line. These were people who wanted to be free of the crippling weight from the lives they were living. Guilty people who want to start over.

Why are you here?

A lifetime ago I used to work in public relations, choreographing events with public officials and minor celebrities. My job was to make them shine in the best light possible, showcasing their accomplishments against a backdrop and with a speech that highlighted how valuable, how important, how distinctly different they were. If I had been planning this event for Jesus, I would have had him standing on the hill, bathed in an aura of light. I would have suggested he call to those people down below, inviting them to turn their eyes upward, forcing them to squint into the sun as they catch a glimpse of him up there on that hill. I certainly wouldn't have had him getting his robe all muddy in a sewer-sludge river.

But Jesus waded in, stared into John's astonished face and told him to go ahead. *This is to reveal God's righteousness.*

Lots of shock value here—but perhaps the biggest shock is that Jesus was willing to be misunderstood, mistaken, to stand in "the sinner's line"—because he was so determined to show that God is *with us*—what the Greeks called Emmanuel. Hebrews called him *'Immānû'ēl*. With all of us, with even the worst of us.

From the very first public appearance in the river to the last public appearance on the cross. There is no place humanity goes that Jesus isn't prepared to go as well.

What a difference from most of the people I know. What a difference from most of the lessons I've been taught. Jesus lived life unencumbered by ego, without vanity, free of the fear of what others might think or do.

The year was 1971, and Walt Disney World had just opened outside Orlando. Florida residents got to preview the park before the grand opening, and my family was going. All of us. And I got to bring a friend.

I knew immediately that I would bring my third grade best friend, Beverly Tinsdale. Beverly and I did pretty much everything together. We went to the same elementary school and did after-school gymnastics together. Beverly spent nights at my house, spending long afternoons swimming and exploring the orange groves surrounding us.

I never saw any differences between Beverly and me. I don't know if my parents ever saw any differences between Beverly and me. If they did, I don't recall them ever saying so.

On that hot day in July of 1971, off we went to Walt Disney World.

And for the first time, I became consciously aware of the fact that Beverly was black. As far as you could see, there were only white people—like me—in the park that day.

The line for the "20,000 Leagues Under the Sea" ride was long, and most of the children had broken ranks, running to play on the large rocks that lined the path. Beverly ran over too. Everyone could see you playing on the rocks. Beverly climbed up to the tallest rock and yelled at me to climb up with her. "You can see the whole park from the top of this!" she called. I just shook my head and stayed in line behind by mother.

It's strange to me how I can still remember Beverly's words: "You don't want to be seen with me, do you?"

You don't want to be seen with me, do you?

My shame came in retrospect.

My regret.

My embarrassment.

My sense of humiliation.

They all came later.

At the time I only recall as a child of eight, being uncomfortable and deeply, deeply self-conscious.

I didn't want to be identified with my best friend, Beverly Tinsdale, because she was black and I was white.

Could I have been any more different from Jesus?

We all have our Beverly stories. Some more dramatic than others. Maybe they are not as dramatic as race. Maybe they are about how someone dresses, their profession, the way they talk. Some of us couldn't have a conversation with a conservative political candidate without belittling and berating. Others have a hard time being friends with a left-leaning, vegan-eating, composting activist without a certain amount of eye-rolling.

Some of us believe it's our right to prove our intellectual prowess by verbal bullying and intellectual sparring—proving ourselves in what we think of as our "tough questions." We like to think we are somehow more rigorous, more curious, deeper than those around us. Some of us hide our moral superiority under good manners and civility. But whatever name we give it—all these little patterns of separation matter. Just as much as they mattered at the Jordan River.

If Jesus could so embrace our humanity and could so identify with us in his baptism, then what's really to stop us from learning to identify with others too?

When Jesus identified with humanity, it wasn't about siding with the Romans against the Jews, the straights against the gays, the fundamentalists against the liberals. Jesus sided with all of us. Or as one of his followers would write just a few decades later: "In Christ there is no Jew or Greek, male or female, slave or free."

Jesus identifies with so that we can identify with him. Or as one of the early church fathers wrote, "Jesus came to us as we are to make us what he is."

The Circle of Reconciliation

As soon as you begin to allow for the possibility that Jesus = God, and that his entire time on earth was spent revealing something precious, about you, me and this world, then it seems the only sensible thing is to lean in and find out a bit more. This, however, may be the time when that loaded six-letter word comes in: *church*. I'll let you determine the adjective you like to put in front of it—over the years many of us have picked up a choice derogative adjective to precede church.

The church should be the brightest institution we have. Jesus originally planned on it being a collection of people who led the kind of life he was leading. In other words, going everywhere and traveling light. This was meant to be a group of people coming alongside the friendless and giving a hand to those who had been taken advantage of. Along the way these followers were supposed to teach and to baptize people who wanted to start a life of something better. Jesus so trusted this vision that he didn't bother writing down his words. He believed his followers were going to remember and reenact his actions and do the one commandment he did give them: "As I have loved you, so love each other."

As I imagine it, the church was like this groovy love bus traveling through the Galilean countryside.

It didn't last long. Within a few decades the movement was becoming a true institution complete with rules, hierarchy, requirements and punishments. And by the time the first century had drawn to a close, great minds were debating the finer points of the gospel. Within a few more centuries the church and the Roman Empire began to overlap as each used the other in a rapid rush to power and acquisition. When Emperor Constantine saw his famous vision (of a cross of light above the sun, which his troops placed on their shields) the merger of church and state was complete. It was official: The power of the state was now harnessing the power of God himself.

Scary.

That's what many of us imagine when we think of the church: a power-drunk institution that in the best of times has forcibly enforced subjective standards of behavior and, in the worst of times, has forcibly stood against the advances of art, science and philosophy, along with compulsively dominating, enslaving and exploiting people.

In one sense the church has danced around with a question many of us know well: How do we hold power, enact power, speak to power, without being seduced, co-opted, destroyed by that same power? The church usually doesn't get it right. And neither do we.

We know that delicious feeling of desiring to be on top. It begins gnawing at us mighty early in life. For the last several years my two younger kids have been in different schools—one in public and one in a private school. I remember when we got socked with a blizzard a few years ago. The snow began late one afternoon and it continued to fall through the night. The next morning every kid in the city of Chicago woke up with one thought on their minds: *Snow Day!*

My thirteen-year-old daughter, Burnley, learned she had a snow day by 7:00 that morning. That's the way private schools operate. The huge bureaucracy of my son's public school system was less nimble. As I dialed the central office line to find out whether they too had called a snow day, I asked her, "Wouldn't it be great if your brother had a day off as well so you guys could play together?"

"Um," she answered. "That would be fun," she said thoughtfully. "But I'd rather watch him go to school while he watches me stay home in my pajamas."

We can relate, can't we? It's a phenomenon called *Schadenfreude*, literally translated from German as "damage joy." The only way I can be sure of my good fortune is to witness your bad fortune. The church, as we all do, struggles with a deep strain of insecurity that defines success by the experience of looking down on someone else.

Things are just that much more enjoyable for us when we are the ones on top. A story came out a few years ago about the famous traveling evangelist Billy Graham. Even Billy Graham couldn't escape the seduction of power! Graham had fifty years of courting and being courted by the most powerful men in the world. Graham counseled eleven presidents and had been close to power for a long time. Long enough that you would think it would lose its magnetic pull.

Yet over the last few years, tapes from his meetings with President Richard Nixon have started surfacing. On more than one occasion, as the disgraced President Nixon began his vile rants against Jewish leaders, the "president's pastor" remained silent.

Graham calls it one of the greatest regrets of his life. There was nothing in Graham that supported anti-Semitism. But as he explains it, he was so seduced by being there, in the Oval Office, sitting with the president, that he lost the courage to speak his convictions. He lost the courage to speak truth. Or as author Michael Duffy put it, "Graham had been so consoling that he had stopped confronting."[1]

How many of us would criticize the lap we sit on? Not many, I suspect. Jesus never forgot what was what; his compass always gave the reading of true north, and he knew that the way to peace and restoration—for us individually and for our world—lay in recovering a sense of neighborliness and protection for ourselves and others.

Jesus knew anytime we use coercion or power to dominate—even in the desire to effect good—we are in danger of being seduced and destroyed by that same power. Jesus wasn't interested in people taking up the cross of Constantine (or the cross of American power for that matter). He was interested in our taking up his cross. The power of the cross was power for creating peace—not power to dominate or bring people to their knees.

The power we're really hungry for—the peace-giving power—is the power of the cross. It's the action of being willing to move from self-protection to self-sacrifice; it's being willing to so identify with the suffering and vulnerability of others that we become vulnerable ourselves.

Peter didn't understand this. The events leading up to the scene of Jesus' transfiguration in Matthew's Gospel narrative has Jesus teaching more and more about his death. Matthew 16:21-22 reads:

> From that time on, Jesus began to show his disciples that he must go to Jerusalem and undergo great suffering at the hands of the elders and chief priests and scribes, and be killed, and on the third day be raised. And Peter took him aside and began to

rebuke him, saying, "God forbid it, Lord! This must never happen to you."

Six days later, Matthew 17 begins, Jesus took Peter, James and John to a mountaintop, and there they got a glimpse of him sheathed in the power and the glory of God. Yet they are the same guys Jesus took with him into the garden of Gethsemane the night before he was taken into Roman custody. Anticipating this, he was troubled, and he asked his friends to stay with him. But they fell asleep.

Follow me in this, Jesus says. *My glory is not going to be held isolated on a mountain, my glory will be found in the agony of the garden, in the sharing of a meal with hungry people. My power will be seen as I move toward those the world marginalizes and tries to ignore.* This is the way of Jesus. This is the power of Jesus. This is how we can begin to imagine effecting real change in the world—in a way that doesn't leave us salivating for the same power the empire-institutions wield.

That's the power that tells the world, *Your problem is my problem.* It's the power that says, *When you suffer, I suffer. When you're thirsty, I'm thirsty too. When you're hungry, I'm hungry.* Imagine going forward in life with this kind of power. Imagine this kind of love.

The cross was the most radical, pro-human, pro-peace message God could give. It was the only message God had for humanity: *I love you, and there's nothing you can do about it. Even killing me won't change my fundamental stance: I am for you.*

We've grown so accustomed to thinking we know what the cross means that we aren't really amazed, astonished or even that curious about it anymore. The earliest church community struggled to make sense of what this cross meant. They asked all kinds of questions:

How could the same power who they believed raised Lazarus from his tomb now be overcome by death himself?

How could the same one who healed the blind men not force his executioners to see him for who he really is?

How could the same power who healed the hemorrhaging woman and cured the sick leper—who had people walking who couldn't walk before, who restored sanity to people called "demoniac" by their community—how was it possible that the source of all this power could be beaten senseless by the whip? Prodded with a Roman baton? Subjected to torture, ridicule and abuse? Bound with rope? Impaled with nails?

How could the source of all that power be so powerless? Limply suspended like a rag doll between heaven and earth? This was an imponderable mystery. This was a "mystery . . . hidden throughout the ages and generations," as the apostle Paul says in his letter to the church at Colossae (Colossians 1:26). It was a mystery into which "angels long to look," Jesus' friend Peter says in his letter to a new group of believers (1 Peter 1:12).

This was the mystery of the cross. The foolishness that confounded the wise. The powerlessness that the religious power taunted. "He saved others; he cannot save himself. He is the King of Israel; let him come down from the cross now, and we will believe in him. . . . Let God deliver him now, if he wants to," as recorded in Matthew 27:42-43. The cross was the wild foolishness of love. To Matthew it looked a lot like the crazy stories Jesus had told him: Stories of a Father who hiked his robes up to his knees and took out across the field to meet his long lost and much beloved baby boy. Stories of an unwelcomed stranger who came across a helpless bleeding man by the roadside and gave his money, his time and his reputation to nurse him to health.

Imagine love that puts itself at the discretion of others. Love that gives the option of loving or not loving in return. Jesus died by surrendering, by showing all his cards, by giving up everything he had to give. Including his life. And letting each one of us do with it what we will.

The cross was the key to everything—it was the key to pushing out all the noise. It silenced all the sirens, all the bleating voices, because it showed for all time this ultimate truth of the universe: God was going to love—no matter what. No matter what it cost, God was determined to *love*.

Love changes everything.

13

Community

The Third Way

*L*ove changed not only my understanding of my life but it continues to change my understanding of our neighbors. The cross points to this mystery—one that runs against the grain of some of our American posturing about independence. The mystery of the cross seems to suggest that our individuality is only made fully complete in relationship with others. It's *the other*, as academics and rabbis sometimes use the term. The rabbi Martin Buber begins his most important work, *I and Thou*, with the understanding that we only know *who we are* by our relationship to those *who are not us*.[1]

It makes sense when you think about it. It's the differences, the comparisons, that allow us to see ourselves as individual and distinct. When we get this self-other relationship out of whack, we use terms like *codependence, diffuse boundaries* and similar language to express something dysfunctional.

What happened on the cross was not just a way of keeping good boundaries; what the cross reveals is a freedom to be *for* others. If we're free from needing to protect ourselves, we are unexpectedly set free to expend our energy in ways that are proactive and intentionally designed for someone else. The cross of Jesus takes an assertive, almost downright aggressive stance in the direction of others. And he gives us the freedom to come alongside and follow him in the same way of being for others.

Free to Share

The apostle Paul talked about this being the work of reconciliation, knitting the parts of something back together so that each part can be whole again. Reconciliation is good for the parts and good for the whole. And it's only possible when people are free enough to share.

I experienced this freedom in an unforgettable way several years ago when I traveled to the far western section of Tanzania in the Maasai Mara, near the Serengeti border. I was with a team of pastors on a mission trip sponsored by World Vision. One hot afternoon a small group of us traveled fifteen minutes or so off road deep into a Maasai community to visit a new water tank—a large concrete holding tank that the government tanker trucks visit every few weeks or so to fill.

The Maasai are very distinctive people, with their long, elegant necks and bright, brilliantly colored—often purple—robes. They typically carry a long walking stick. Frankly, they are the poster children for *National Geographic*.

The Maasai were once the most feared warriors on the continent. Now they largely scramble for food at every opportunity. We drove further and further into the hills when we suddenly came upon a row of donkeys and women walking with their children and countless yellow plastic jugs all making their way to the water tank.

The Maasai men were waiting for us. All arranged in a circle on benches that they had carried on foot from the local school miles away. They proudly showed us their water tank and, through gestures, explained how it worked. Then they carefully arranged us at the benches and in slow and carefully worded Swahili told us what this water tank meant to their lives, their families.

Our translator, a Maasai man himself, was moved to tears. Then without any warning the leader burst into a wide smile and said he wanted to celebrate with us. Out from behind a row of donkeys they very proudly brought some bottled sodas they had lugged from town. Sodas! Something they themselves had very rarely tasted. They stood, straight-backed and tall as they passed these warm bottles out to us.

Then the women started their cries. The high sound of *la-la-la-la-la* pierced the air, and three men made their way to us with the greatest luxury they could offer. They had killed a goat that morning. A delicacy they may eat once a month at most had been killed in our honor. Freshly roasted a few hours earlier—the legs of the goat were sticking out of five-gallon buckets the men carried with great dignity.

I was both honored and horrified. The reality began to sink in: This leg, with a hoof still attached and flies swarming all over it, was meant *for me.* They drove stakes into the ground, and the leg—complete with singed hair, was skewered on it. With a machete knife the men cut pieces to share with us.

They were giving us the finest of what they had, sharing the very best. This fresh goat wasn't from their excess; it really cost the Maasai villagers to share with us.

In the silence of our van ride back to the main road, one of the guys spoke up: "It's a humbling thing when hungry people share what they have."

Being with food-insecure people—hungry people—who are free to share what they have is something unforgettable. Most people I know, myself included, are so focused on acquiring and then defending our acquisitions that we have a difficult time even imagining what it would be like to live differently. If one of my kids brings home an unexpected dinner guest, I wonder how often my first inclination is to say, "No problem!" (Not often.) Or after work, I may drive by the field to pick up my son or daughter from a sporting practice that went a little bit longer than expected. I no doubt had to wait a while, and I'm usually tired, thinking about how I still have to cook dinner when I get home. Then the car door opens, and there are several more students alongside them, wondering if they can get a ride home as well, since they are "on the way." Day to day, just how free to share am I?

The cross offers us a way of holding it all loosely. And I do mean *all*. Our time, our energy, our jobs, our possessions. Holding it loosely enough that we can stop defending and protecting them all the time. Holding them loosely enough that we might just start enjoying them again.

Practices of Restoration

"Holding it loosely" was one of the most striking characteristics of the first church communities. They were free enough to share what they had with each other. These early followers of the Way, as they were called, began caring for the weakest around them in ways that were startling and new. They shared their crops and the proceeds of their crops with others who were hungry; they made clothes and shared what they had made with those who had need; they made room in their homes and at their tables for those who needed a place to sleep and a plate to eat. This was *koinōnia*. This Greek word translates as meaning a distinctive far-reaching commonality toward others. The world had never seen it before.

The practice of *koinōnia* was about as far as one could go from the typical trigger-ready, self-protecting boundaries most of us are accustomed to setting up. Like the boundaries we set up when we feel we're being pushed to our limits.

A person recently told me that they were drawing a "line in the sand." I thought about how elusive "lines in the sand" actually are.

In the fine sands of the desert, you drag your toe to draw the pro-
verbial line and simply watch as seconds later the constantly shifting
sand fills in the narrow crevice you had just drawn.

I remember one of my own line-in-the-sand experiences. It was a
midweek summer night and the hot weather had suddenly and unexpectedly turned cool. I had opened all the windows in the house
earlier before everyone went to bed. Before turning in I specifically
asked one of my kids to prop open the bathroom door, knowing that
in the stiff breeze, the door would bang open and shut. I'm a pretty
light sleeper and I knew I would hear it in the night otherwise.

We all went to bed.

I woke up around one thirty in the morning to a loud bang. Yep.
The bathroom door had not been propped open, and the wind from
the west was knocking it hard. Just like I predicted. I lay there for a
few minutes sleepily thinking, *Shoot. I have to go down and prop it
open.* But my next thought was, *No. Let the door wake them up! I'm
sick of being the designated maid around here. Their bedrooms are
right next to the bath. The door knocking on the wall is going to be
much louder for them. I'll let them wake up and handle it.*

So I pulled the pillow over my head and eventually fell back
asleep. Then I woke up at three. More banging. I rooted around
until I found some earplugs, and then, fully awake, I forced myself to
go back to sleep.

You think I'm small, don't you? Well, yeah, I know that. But I had
made a decision. This far and no further! I had laid down the law,
drawn my line in the sand. Under most circumstances, my kids
would have felt the ramifications of that line.

Unfortunately for me, everyone else in my family is a very sound
sleeper. At four thirty the ridiculousness of it all and my own weariness was too much. I gave in. I went down, propped the door open,
returned to bed and immediately fell into a sound sleep.

It was silly. Stupid really. It was just a line in the sand.

We all draw lines someplace. Where do you do it?

Do you do it at work? With your partner? *That's it! I'm not picking up after you anymore!* You can bet we do it at church! *If they don't start singing some hymns/using the organ/having more praise music (fill in the blank), then I'm done with it!*

It's not that some lines aren't important. The lines that outline our boundaries are elements in defining appropriate responsibility or roles. But sometimes what our lines actually define is our unwillingness to change, to adapt.

If we're not careful, those lines we draw—those boundaries—can be the beginning of a wall.

American culture rewards people who are firm, resolute. People who stand like tall trees, independent and proud. People who are impervious to the impressions of others. People who say what they mean, mean what they say and stick to it.

But we are not designed to be tall trees, independent and proud. God calls us into community. And community is messy. It's not about *I'm sticking to my guns! This far and no farther! I've said it for the last time, and I really mean it!* Community is about collaboration, engagement, trust and togetherness.

Many of us know just how far statements like "I've said it for the last time" get us in our marriages. Relationships aren't about drawing lines in the sand, and communities can never be built on borders that began as lines drawn in the sand.

We are going to be tempted to keep drawing lines if we don't really understand that God redeems people in order to call them into community with each other. And in community with each other we are called to bend, change, adjust and adapt. Remember the story of the outcast woman who came to the well in the middle of the day? After Jesus tells her about the "living water," she immediately runs and tells her community what happened to her so that they can experience it for themselves. Do you recall the man who lived among the tombs?

When Jesus restores the man to himself, he virtually begs to leave in the boat with Jesus, but the Son of God stops him by saying, "Return to your people, tell them what has happened to you." The bleeding woman is restored in the presence of people, thereby removing her shame and restoring her to her rightful place in the community; the adulterous woman is told to "go home and sin no more"—and we can assume Jesus believed she would have a home, a place, a community to which she could go. With Jesus, it's about community—relationships—trusting and accepting each other. Again and again.

Community is a concept that gets real practical really fast. Perhaps that's why there is so much talk throughout the entire Bible about what we do with our material resources—because being in community with others is not just about talking about it but actually living it. It was the very practical way love was made visible by giving and sharing that caused the Roman empire to take notice of this small band of fledging believers. "Behold how they love one another!"[2] Just like the Maasai men slaughtering and sharing the prized goat, it's concrete sharing that makes it real.

Remember that story Jesus told about the shepherd who went out looking for the one sheep? Jesus opens that parable using the phrase, "Suppose one of you . . ." Suppose *one of you*! Suppose one of you had a sheep who got lost? In other words, suppose one of you starts looking at the people around you and feels a tug on the rope? Suppose one of you starts to look out for each other, going out into the night to find the one who has wandered off, or carefully staying up late to make sure the "sheep" have a place to stay and food to eat?

Suppose one of you. Perhaps one of you who doesn't even think you're so special or significant or important in any way at all begins to act like you have a responsibility to those around you? Suppose you begin to act like a shepherd!

Jesus is speaking, perhaps, too poetically. It was up to his followers to make it practical.

Suppose one of you decided to leave the comfort of the familiar—the ninety-nine—and you go out to befriend the one who is struggling, who is different, who is on his or her own.

Or suppose one of you decided that the ninety-nine other things you had to do can wait to attend to the one you encounter in the coffee shop. Or the distraught neighbor who's walking his dog. Or the coworker who is worried about her son.

Suppose one of you begins to see that community isn't complete unless all of the lost and the lonely are befriended.

The world is dying for us to make reconciliation practical. Just think about our environment for a minute. When I really accept that I am responsible for our environment, things start to change.

For instance, just to return to that hot, dusty day deep in the Maasai Mara, seeing myself as a shepherd reminds me that the average person in Tanzania uses only two gallons of water a day and that 43 percent of them walk at least half a mile to get that water. This small detail must not be lost on me as I use the American standard of eighty to one hundred gallons each day. While I run the water tap waiting on the water to get warm, I am not allowed to lose sight of the fact that in the African continent six thousand children will die from drinking unsafe water or from poor sanitation. That's a little more than four children per minute.

While I'm running the laundry on the gentle cycle—for just a few of the delicate clothes—I remember talking to a thirteen-year-old girl in Kisongo who gets up at dawn to walk the thirty minutes to the well, hoping she can get back in time to still make the walk to school. And I remember her shyly telling me about the number of former classmates who were raped in the pre-dawn hours and found themselves pregnant and soon married off. All because they didn't have a well closer to home.

No, I can't ignore that fact while I'm running my bath or fueling my car or eating beef (again!) at dinner. If I'm going to really enter the community of God's people, then I have to be fully in. That's the only way I am able to give and to receive the full benefits of reconciliation.

Doing It Together and Not Doing It All

I can imagine how you might start to sweat when you hear words like responsibility and proactive compassion. I get that. I start to sweat too. Meeting all of the needs of the whole world is a scary undertaking.

But meeting all of the needs of the whole world isn't our job. While he was walking around on the earth, Jesus made it pretty clear that filling all the needs wasn't his job either. Mark's Gospel (the first one written among the Gospel narratives) records a story in his opening chapter that made it very clear that Jesus wasn't planning on meeting all the needs that came to him.

On the surface it seems like a simple story. After being baptized, Jesus went out into the desert for forty days, where he came face to face with evil. One of the first things he did when he returned was to go to his friend Peter's house. Stop for a minute and place this in your mind: After forty days of sleeping outside, solitary, as he fasted and prayed, Jesus went into a home! Home. That place of peace and refuge, that place that conjures up images of safety, quiet intimacy and needed rest.

Jesus enjoyed his sabbath there, but beginning at sundown, the text takes on a different tone—a conflictual tone. Needs begin to emerge in that home of peace and tranquility.

As soon as the sun went down, people started crawling out of the darkness—all looking to be healed. Ragged people. Sick people. People being carried by their relatives. Fathers tearfully bringing their sick sons and daughters, leading their addled mothers by the hand.

They kept coming and coming and coming. Until, as Mark described it, "the whole city was gathered around the door" (Mark 1:33).

Jesus healed many, Mark remembers. But the next morning Jesus slipped away undetected. You want conflict? You've got it right here. Here are the disciples who have just signed on with Jesus. He has healed some people—even a family member! (What a nice perk.) The word is leaking out, there is some buzz about him, and then without warning they wake up to find him gone.

The disciples, irritated, looked for Jesus. That's the force of the Greek word *katadiōkō.* They pursued him; they hunted him down.

And who can blame them? I mean it's great for Jesus to go away and pray, but Peter is the one who has some angry men in his face! Worried fathers see Peter's mother-in-law walking around healed while their own sons are dying of a fever.

Why heal any if you're not going to heal all, Jesus! The disciples didn't understand, and when they caught up with Jesus, they were annoyed and frustrated.

What are you doing here? Peter asks. *There's a whole village dying outside my mother-in-law's door. It's obvious—you've got to go back and heal them!* But Jesus didn't buy that. He knew there would always be more needs than he—or they—would be able to respond to. But he also understood the great temptation his followers would have to try and do it all.

Jesus gave them *a third way.* He showed them a way of living open and responsive to the pressing needs of the world in a self-directed manner. Jesus took his own cues from God, his Father, and showed them that they could do that too. And not only that, they could trust each other in following that same divine direction. Jesus shows his disciples what an *interdependent model of community* looks like.

Jesus had in his mind a way of acting in the world that the disciples couldn't yet understand, but they decided to trust him. And when Jesus explained to them, "We must leave here," the disciples decided to trust Jesus and the community he was building.

It was a different way of responding to the world's illness and needs. Jesus returned in trust to his Father, and then he turned and trusted the disciples to carry out the task of building community in the world.

This is a way of reconciliation that allows each of us the freedom to live uniquely in the places we were called to and live the lives we were meant to live. I don't have to try to tell you what you should be doing! That's not my job. And your job isn't to tell me. Our responsibilities, however, are to be faithful and responsive to the needs God does call us to meet. No one person among us can meet all the needs we see, but we can each meet some.

A Quaker friend of mine gave me an illustration that has stayed with me. She likens the tasks of community to a journey through a forest. Along the path there are bundles of sticks travelers are expected to pick up and move along. Some are to burn as firewood, other bundles are brush that is being cleared away, and others are simply things that need to be adjusted. Travelers are expected to carry only one at a time. But all bundles are expected to be moved. So the ones who come early and pick up the bundles at the beginning have to trust that those who come after them will pick up the ones farther down the path. Those travelers who drop their bundles after carrying them as far as they can have to rely on someone farther behind them to pick them back up again. The bundles are moved through the forest because everyone leans in and does just what is asked of them.

Jesus came to "seek out and to save the lost," but his actions didn't depend on external provocation (see Luke 19:10). Jesus' actions flowed from his knowledge of who he was and what he came to do. He realized that he wasn't called to heal everyone. But he was bringing the good news of God to a group of followers—people who were individually being prepared to go on and be healers—proclaimers of the good news.

Jesus was content to build his church, what Paul will call "his body," trusting those people (see 1 Corinthians 12). Knowing that those people were all going to reach points of irritation. They would have points of disagreement, points of consternation, points when they fought over what to do and how to do it.

Let me give you an image of what this third way looks like. Because it's the way we can respond and live as the church—the body—that Jesus was building. The third way looks like the guy next to you praying for you when you are too weak to pray for yourself—even though one of you is walking the canoe and another is on the rapids. When you're exhausted and don't know where to turn, you still know the person next to you is praying for you.

The third way looks like some of us being activists when others of us can't be. You have to recognize that there are many issues you will remain ignorant of. There are many pressing prayers you will rarely pray, many opportunities to help that you will not see. Being on the third way is a way of trusting that in the big picture all these concerns and all these prayers are being addressed. And you don't have to do them all. You can be confident that someone (perhaps not you) is working for women's rights in Kurdistan. And that someone is standing alongside young girls being abducted into the sex traffic trade in Burma. Someone is praying by name for the homeless in Kashmir, and someone else is working for the rights of the undocumented workers in Alabama. All these things are happening.

You and I are not personally called to meet all the needs and pray all the prayers, but we are called to meet and pray for some. That's our responsibility.

Ultimately the church that Jesus had in mind isn't a group of people standing straight up; we are a group of people all leaning in. Leaning in toward each other. Borrowing what we need for the moment from the person on our right and our left. At times, borrowing our sister's joy when we feel joyless and using another's faith when we are faithless.

The church of Jesus is a group of people living not in the dichotomy of "my way or the highway," but in a third way, turning and trusting the ones around us as we trust the direction of God.

14

Little Choices

It's All Little Choices

Almost two decades ago I had a near death experience. Eighteen years sounds like so long ago. But if I get in the right frame of mind it's still fresh. It should be—I've prayed almost daily that I would remember the details as clear-eyed as possible.

It was Wednesday morning and I was home in our one-bedroom apartment with our toddler, Sumner. I woke up feeling miserable, got worse as the morning went on, and while fixing Sumner a snack, the pain in my abdomen was so gripping that I slipped to the floor. I called a girlfriend who was a nurse and gave her my symptoms wondering if it was a ruptured appendix or something.

She was at the apartment door in fifteen minutes. Sumner had to open it for her. By the time we got to the ER at Northwestern, I couldn't stand up. I was sweaty and a little delusional. They shortly had me in an exam room, where they began running tests, asking me questions and trying to determine what was going on. They knew there was some internal bleeding. I was losing a lot of blood. But they didn't know what was causing it.

Within a half hour I was being prepped for surgery. My husband got there just a few seconds before they took me into the operating room. Then I blacked out.

When I became conscious, the room was a madhouse. The white coats were rushing around; the doctor I had met in the ER was yelling into the phone, "The patient has seized! I need somebody down here STAT." The anesthesiologist was hovering around my head. And I thought, *I'm going to die. There was no problem with me yesterday, today something serious has happened. They don't know what it is. They won't get it in time.*

My card is punched.

Even though I knew I was dying, I still wanted some confirmation on it. So I asked them, "I'm going to die, aren't I?" Over and over, I kept asking because no one was answering me. For this drama to be about me, I felt like I was being completely ignored. *Can you just tell me—I'm dying, aren't I?*

And finally the anesthesiologist took my chin and firmly, impatiently, even a little angrily I thought, said, "You are not going to die! Quit saying that!"

Well, now I knew for sure I was going to die. But quietly. I was going to go quietly. One thing you don't want to do is tick off the doctors along the way.

For the next window of time I laid in the ER and thought about my life. I could remember no Scripture passages. At all. I even tried to recite "The Lord is my shepherd . . ." but then I was stuck. Just *where* was it he was supposed to lead me? Still waters? Green pastures? The *valley of death!?*

I gave up on the Scriptures. Instead I tried to pray, but I couldn't focus on praying. So instead I started doing an inventory of my life. I was twenty-nine years old and I realized with a start just how precious every single one of those years had been. What had I done with them? Had I done anything that was going to last?

Maybe something like that has happened to you.

You have that sudden recognition that few are the days. And life really is a candle in the wind. The present moment is always giving way to the future, and most days that future is the following sunrise. Sunday evening steps aside to make room for Monday morning. Until the day it doesn't step aside. And the future isn't the next morning; it's the last breath.

Ernest Becker wrote the classic book *The Denial of Death*. It's not exactly an upper, but he describes the paradox of humanity in a way that cuts to the chase:

> Man is literally split in two: he has an awareness of his own splendid uniqueness in that he sticks out of nature with a towering majesty, and yet he goes back into the ground a few feet in order blindly and dumbly to rot and disappear forever. It is a terrifying dilemma. . . .
>
> We are . . . gods with anuses.[1]

Gods with anuses. Now that's a phrase you don't forget too quickly.

We are such terrifying, precious people. We are bearers of such deep mysteries that even angels long to know (1 Peter 1:12). But we are people equally made of the same dirt to which we will one day return.

Throughout this book I've tried to describe the various ways we rush forward or fall back as we seek to become the real us—the authentic us: people who are in the process of being put back together, of being made new.

Repeatedly being put back together comes down to the little choices. The small decisions.

I lay in that hospital room—certain of death, wondering about my twenty-nine years. I became increasingly confident: I felt sure that God was in all and was all. Even as I thought about the two people I loved most in this world, my husband and my precious son,

I had a peace that was indescribable. I knew with rock certainty that they were going to be okay.

They were undergirded by a bottomless river of *eternal love*. Sumner would grow up to be marvelous. Terry—after what I hoped would be a decade in mourning—would be just fine too.

And me? I knew the end was going to be okay. All that fear of death that grips you in the middle of the night—really stopped for me when I thought I was actually dying. I was convinced that in the end . . . there was God.

We need not fear death! How many of us have broken out in a cold sweat about it? The "Big D" in the basement. The terror residing in the closet. I didn't see any white light, but I did have a complete conviction that God is the eternal bedrock.

No. I didn't have concerns about dying. Instead, just before the anesthesiologist put me to sleep, I found myself regretting two things about how I'd lived in those twenty-nine years. One was a writing project I had wanted to attempt. A project I really wanted to do. But I was so uncertain about my abilities, so insecure about whether it would be successful, that I never even tried to do it. I was profoundly sad about that. In that moment of clarity I realized that being successful wasn't the point. The fear of failing had kept me from even trying.

And second, a week or so earlier I had been asked to speak at a woman's retreat. Maybe fifty or so women, on a topic close to my heart: hospitality. I wanted to say yes, but I had said no. Speaking in front of people was terrifying. And what if I couldn't say something meaningful?

I had had invitations, opportunities to *live*. I had been given opportunities to be part of the big story of God, but I had turned away. My fears were keeping me small.

Since then I have been given a few glimpses of all the ways people live large by the smallest of decisions. How they live eternally when they are willing to step out in the smallest of ways. A few years ago I was touched by a terrible accident involving a teenager who for weeks hung suspended between life and death.

The accident happened on a Sunday night, and no one knew if Richard Smith was even going to survive the night. As soon as I got the news I left for the forty-minute trip to a suburban hospital, making a few quick phone calls en route.

I was calling a few people to pray. Specifically I was calling those people who I knew would put down the phone and get down on their knees as soon as they heard my message. By 9 a.m. on the following Monday I had a voice message from one of these praying people. It was from a Ph.D. student who had been largely sequestered for months while she finished her dissertation. She was calling just to let me know that on Sunday—hours before the accident—she had a strong sense that she was being directed to pray for the Smith family.

"Let them know," she said, "let them know the Spirit had already called people forth."

The nudge to pray for others is something so small most of the time, isn't it? Almost unnoticed for many of us. And yet . . . and yet. It's enormous when you imagine that this nudge might be the mechanism by which power, strength, courage and comfort enter into others and connect us one to another.

In a similar way with the same family emergency, a few days later I was hurriedly leaving the office to visit Richard at the hospital when someone gave me a wad of money and whispered, "Give it to the Smiths."

I was happy to do this. I knew that there were a lot of needs. I knew that Richard's older brother Sam and his wife were spending the week at the hospital. Sam was in graduate school and his wife, Debra, had taken a week off work. A week they couldn't really afford financially.

So I wasn't surprised, when after handing the money to Richard's dad, he asked me if it would be okay if he just gave it to Sam and

Debra. Sure, I said. It wasn't for any specific purposes. When they counted it, Debra sat still for a minute then said, "This is, to the dollar, my salary for a week."

I might find that story strange if I didn't hear is so frequently. This is just the kind of invitation God gives to people. Little decisions, little choices, that set in motion something so much bigger.

When you're undone you can be in a place of wondering if anything really matters. But as you start to be knit back together, you realize a lot of that work is simply being willing to believe that there is a deeper force, a deeper power at work. The nudge is an invitation. Kind of like the invitation John experienced thousands of years ago when out of an apocalyptic vision, a rush of scenes, dangers and future events, God spoke a clear resounding word of clarity to an aged warrior. A disciple who wanted to be known only as the "one loved by the Lord," who now lived a lonely exile on the island of Patmos.

John was a man staring at his own death. A man sitting with his own particular regrets, his own unique doubts, his own worries, likely doing his own life inventory of some sort. He had a vision that still causes people to cover their mouths in horror. Violent overthrows, weeping mothers and warring factions. There is no place death has not touched.

While this cinematic terror plays behind him, John hears a word uttered by God himself. And what a word it is. John sees a city descending from heaven. It's glittering. Beautiful. *Wait a minute*, he thinks, *I've seen this place before. These are streets I've walked. These are doorways I've passed.*

He recognizes it and at the same time doesn't. This is Jerusalem. Except it's a Jerusalem that has only have been imagined in dreams. John sees the City of Peace, the City of God, but without the warfare that characterized it on earth. He sees it as God had dreamed of it. Filled with all sorts of nationalities, a bustling civic space with people living together in community. This is the city God always wanted it to be: Jerusalem redeemed! And undergirding all of this is the power of the God whom John had described as *love* (see Revelation 21).

This is what it looks like for love to dwell with humankind.

See, John! I am making all things new. Write this down, John. I am the Alpha and the Omega, the beginning and the end (Revelation 21:5-6).

In the end, John, there is just what the world began with: me. The I AM who formed order from chaos. Who spoke creation into existence, who established the earth on its axis and separated the day from the night. In the end it all returns to me. It is done, John. Behold, I am making all things new. I am going to take it all, the work of human hands, the hopes you've had, the relationships you've cultivated, I'm going to take it all, and I'm going to make it new. Fresh. Revitalized.

I'm not making all new things. I'm making all things new.

God doesn't erase it all, starting from scratch. God takes what remains, what you and I have done, what our parents and our grandparents have done, and uses that to begin building. Just the way God used the physical buildings of Jerusalem to show John what the New Jerusalem was eventually going to become.

It's like God leans over and sees our families, our hopes, our dreams, our actions, and says, *Now, let's see how it was supposed to be all along, shall we?*

You know, the Spirit is just as present in your life as it was in John's life. The Spirit is just as relevant in your life as the Spirit was in those clustered around Richard throughout those weeks. The Spirit is communicating to you just as much as to me. Your response is just as important, just as far-reaching, just as potentially life-changing as any person who has ever lived.

Some of us are at an age where we're feeling settled and on a fixed path. Certainly, some of us are beyond the time when we would do something crazy. Our patterns are set; our routines are firmly established. You are not looking for anything new every morning. Can you begin to imagine that it's just possible that there are one or two great adventures still in you? Might there be some new friends to make? Some new habits to start? Some fresh ideas to act on? Can you still listen to the nudge of the Spirit—even when you think it doesn't matter?

Or maybe you are right there on the cusp. You're fresh out of college. Ready to make your mark. You've got a plan—all successful people have a plan, you think. Have you left room for something to come out of left field and absolutely arrest you? Have you kept yourself open for the God who interrupts? The Voice that calls? The Spirit that carries you in an uncharted direction?

Or maybe you're walking a hard road already. Times are tough. You're struggling with health conditions or buried in debt or dealing with unemployment. *Follow a new road? Are you kidding? I'm just trying to survive!*

Can you believe that the Spirit right now is whispering, guiding, directing? Can you listen—even when it doesn't make sense?

Or maybe your life is like mine right now. Or my husband's life. You have serious responsibilities. A lot of people are depending on you. You need to come through for them. It seems hard to respond to something out of the ordinary. Can you have the courage, even now, to pull up the tent stakes, to step on a desert road, on the basis of a prompting from the Spirit? Or maybe you're where I was on the worst—and best—day of my life. Your confidence is shot. You have no credibility and no way of seeing past your shame and your failures to how this life ever gets better. Can you find the will to listen for the Spirit of God among all the voices that tell you how hopeless it is? Can you hear that insistent Voice that's been telling you, *You don't have to live like this?*

It all starts with little choices. Little choices to pay attention. To lean in and listen. The little choice to stand up. To take a step. And another step. And start walking down a desert road. Now.

In the end the only song will be the one the world opened with when the first brilliant rays of sun appeared. It will be the song of the Alpha and the Omega. The holy Lamb of God who has painfully absorbed all of the suffering we've inflicted, all the bloody bodies left by war. And to all those timid ones—all of us—who have sat at traffic lights wishing we could just step out and do one thing great. I think God's saying, *Go ahead. Go ahead and live like you believe it. I'm with you every step of the way. Right until the very end.*

15

The Arc of the Future

*T*he image lingered long after the words. The sad certainty bringing tears to his eyes, the fatigue and conviction pressing down his slumped shoulders. Weariness puddled around our table at the crowded coffee shop.

"I only know one thing for sure," David said. "My old life doesn't fit any longer. I can't go back there. I can't *be* back there." He was nearing fifty, an accomplished professional singer and teacher. And for the first time in twelve years, he was asking himself the question: *Do I want to keep living like this?*

David was undone. I knew the terrain well. *Do I want to keep living like this?* Answering the question wasn't easy. To even ask that question takes some courage, but to make a change when your life is framed around an entirely different answer—that takes desperate conviction. David was prepared to do it because he had a sense that *some thing—some one*—was calling him out and asking him to walk in the searing light of the sun.

But what a toll that walk in the sun was going to take. I sat with David in the shadow of the coffee shop while he named all the painful choices he would have to face from this day forward. He was going to have to form a new sort of relationship with his wife and grown children. He would need to establish a new relationship with Jesus, the one who came to "make all things new," as he asked new questions about his faith, entertained different possibilities as to how God leads and works in our lives. To embark on a new life was going to require him to live intentionally and consciously for the first time in a long while.

Awake, Alert and Aware

Nearly two thousand years after Jesus lived, the British writer C. S. Lewis suggested that with each decision we make, all throughout our days, we are slowly turning into a heavenly creature or a fiendish one. "There are no *ordinary* people. You have never talked to a mere mortal."[1] All day long we are faced with little things that seem so insignificant, subtle distortions, small pockets of pride, a cup of control or power, a heaping spoonful of fear that causes us to turn away. Choice by choice, our lives are being formed and made.

But the patterns of our lives are so ingrained—the regularity of our habits so unnoticed or unexamined—that we easily move from action to action. We go from home to work and home again without consciously deciding much of anything beyond what we want to eat for lunch or what we're going to watch on television. Like a long pattern of front yard driveways, filled with children dribbling the balls in unison, unthinking, unblinking, unaware, we keep doing what we're doing.

Over the years I've watched these patterns in my own life and in the dear people in our community. In one home I observed a husband who dutifully returned home at the same time each evening, then settled into the easy chair watching five hours of television each night, living in a fantasy world so he wouldn't have to relate to the people in his own family who love and want his presence with them.

In other homes I've watched parents push their kids from early reading programs to preschool math enrichment programs—all from a deep fear that their sons or daughters won't measure up. But they never stop to ask where those yardsticks of measurement came from.

To change course would mean we have to face what those impulses are really all about.

We'd have to pay attention to all the ways we justify and defend our egos—not only in those neon moments of failure—but in so many smaller, more nuanced ways. It's *me* when I defend my position first and listen to the other side second. It's *you* when you lash out at the smallest of criticisms.

It's all the stuff *we* don't face, but it's also the inexpressible, unbearable grace that we miss. It's the time when your child wants you to linger just a little bit longer at the art table, but you're stressed about the next thing on the list. When we hurry through the storybook at night because we're just too tired.

It's also we who refuse to take our place at the table. We who refuse to accept the worth and dignity God has created us with. So we absorb the blows of words or the physical blows because we have this broken core that says we deserve this.

Being on autopilot is not unique. It's our default switch. What's unusual is being the one who stops and asks the question, *Is this how I want to live?*

Waking up is the first step of awareness. Be aware. You have a choice.

As we sat and talked, it was clear that David knew he had a choice, but was he willing to make the change those choices would require?

When I was first installed as a pastor at LaSalle Street Church I prayed this prayer that Paul had prayed for the church community at Ephesus. He wrote,

I have heard of your faith in the Lord Jesus and your love

toward all the saints, and for this reason I do not cease to give thanks for you as I remember you in my prayers. I pray that the God of our Lord Jesus Christ, the Father of glory, may give you a spirit of wisdom and revelation as you come to know him, so that, with the eyes of your heart enlightened, you may know what is the hope to which he has called you, what are the riches of his glorious inheritance among the saints, and what is the immeasurable greatness of his power for us who believe, according to the working of his great power. (Ephesians 1:15-19)

I asked our church to know that God is always, at every moment, bringing something new into being. It was a prayer for continual transformation. Conversion that is ongoing. It was a plea that we would become increasingly like Jesus and that we would, as a community, always be pressing forward to what lies ahead.

Nine years later it's still the prayer I pray. But with a bit more experience, personally and pastorally. The longer I serve in ministry and the older I get, the more aware I am of how difficult it is to live in this place Paul prayed for. What we know about God on one day—even our experience of God on a given day—we often doubt the next day.

And the hope we have, this future expectation of what God is doing, can sometimes seem fragile and fleeting. And the power that Paul talked about, the same power capable of blowing open the door of a tomb and raising the dead, can be reduced to a desperate plea for parking places and safe travels.

My prayer that my church community might always be in a place of ongoing conversion and transformation has been the most vexing of all. Because continual transformation really means living in a tension between who we are now and who we are becoming. And living in that tension, on many days, is not glorious or sexy or fun. Living in that tension is, well, tense. Friction is bound to happen when the past, the present and the emerging future rub shoulders with one another.

My family recently celebrated two milestones, both wonderful. Both offered an excellent example of colliding past, present and future.

My oldest son graduated from college, and my second son, Porter, graduated from high school. Here they are, blossoming young adults. Becoming capable, competent people in the world. Or I should say, they're on that road. But I still call my son Porter by the name I gave him as an infant. Each night when I head for bed, I fight the urge to say, "Good night, Squeezie!" Most nights, I catch myself. But not always. And when I forget, the icy coldness of Porter's immediate response — "Don't call me that, Mom" — punctures any cozy maternal thoughts I harbored.

Much to his horror, my son will always be "Squeezie" to me. But to thrive, to live, he has to be something beyond that as well. A future somebody I see with the memory of the past and the reality of the present. Somebody with that well-researched teenage-reptilian brain still hanging on, but sharing space with this emerging person of the future. *And if I can't enter that space, then something important about our relationship begins to die, doesn't it?*

Paul's prayer to the church at Ephesus is a prayer to a group of people who knew something powerful about the past. They were a group of Gentiles. They were people who had been estranged, outliers, enemies. They had spent years wearing a different face, a different mask. In the city of Ephesus, a sophisticated metropolis along a well-established trade route, it is likely these folks had spent years chasing riches and importance. And Paul begins by reminding them of this past before also reminding them of the present. Listen again, he says, to what God says about you: You are *chosen. Destined. Released. Forgiven. Sons and daughters.* This past and this present are important for the central reason that they are the starting point for a future God is bringing them into. The whole arc of the Bible is distinguished by a dynamic of straining forward. God will stop at nothing short of all-out redemption.

Throughout the stories of the Bible God is consistently seeing people simultaneously as who they are right now *and* who they are emerging to be. Designed to be. Destined to be.

Where others saw Sarah as a barren old woman, God saw her as the matriarch of a great nation. Where some viewed him as a stuttering orphan or a lucky refugee, God saw Moses as the leader who will be used to free a nation. Where his father, Jesse, and his brothers only saw an awkward teenaged shepherd, God saw David as the man to restore the nation of Israel.

And where the disciple could only see his failure, Jesus was already promising Peter that his future meant that he would be the rock (from the literal Greek *Petra*) on which the church would be built.

God sees us as we are. And at the very same time, God sees our past choices and why we made them and where they may lead—what was bad, what was even worse and what was good. God takes it all and puts it to use right this second, using it all to reveal what our future could be.

God sees who we are becoming—what is being called forth. God sees the arc of the future, happening every second as the present moment gives way to the next moment. *There . . . now there . . . now there . . .* as the present continues to step aside to receive the emerging future.

God dwells in this place of tension and asks us to dwell in it as well.

To live in that place means we have to do the hard work of letting go of the past in order to embrace the future—at every opportunity. I know what it costs. That doesn't prevent me from longing to still have this wonderful version of myself simply arrive at the door by UPS. *I want the outcome, but can't I be spared the hardness, the fatigue, the discipline of getting there?* Can't we be spared the tension?

No. We can't.

And in my experience neither can we do this kind of work alone, in isolation. We need others to do this with us. People who can encourage the new and witness the passing of the old.

We need the church. And by that I mean, the *community* of the church: a group of people committed and bearing witness to the reality of *now, but not yet*. A group of people who don't pontificate or judge or correct. A group of people whose first instinct is to have your back. That's right. People who say, *We have your back*. A church where people are committed to loving you as you emerge into something new.

Because to become new people, we have to be free enough to fail. And so does everyone else.

The church that Jesus imagined is one where everybody gets a second chance and a third chance, and fiftieth and hundredth chances. It's a place that doesn't make sense from the outside. Where the way up is to be a servant, where we unleash power not through flexing our strength, but through exposing our vulnerabilities. Where people are willing to risk investing in one another because more than anything they want that large future they have sensed on the horizon out ahead of them. They want to be people leaning forward with the sun in their face and the wind at their back, eager and expectant.

Tension and Transformation

Life in this place of tension is what the Bible is all about. These are the people who inhabit its pages. We too easily treat the Bible like some kind of basic instruction manual. It's not. Treating the Bible like it's an exam review sheet where you can simply memorize the answers to a cosmic test makes a mockery of these texts.

To be engaged with the message of transformation means we engage with the people and stories of this book and ask ourselves what does this living and active word mean? This word that's "sharper than any two-edged sword" (Hebrews 4:12). *This word that penetrates right to our core and divides soul and spirit, joints and marrow, as it judges the thoughts and attitudes of the heart.* When was the last time you really listened to this Word? And wrestled with it? Engaged with it? When was the last time you heard the quiet, comforting Word of a living God speak from the poetry of the Psalms? Or heard the disquieting speech of the prophets challenging your own sacred cows?

To risk being changed personally is to risk simultaneously being changed as a society as well. The perspective of the Bible is that the personal sphere cannot be divided from the social sphere. God's devotion is to this world—to each person and to the whole. So whatever question we are debating in the public square, you can trust that the Bible speaks to it.

Immigration? This book talks about the stranger among us. It doesn't provide us with a road map of where Republicans and Democrats fall out. It provides a framework for how to articulate the issues as God sees them.

Economic divisions and income inequality? The news media readily shares that one out of every seven persons in the United States slipped into poverty during the economic crisis that began in 2008. It grew to the highest rate in fifteen years. This text has something to say about the yawning economic chasms that divide us.

The Bible is relevant and real, and the people who inhabit its pages are people who have faced what you and I face. Life has disappointed them, others have disappointed them, and they have disappointed themselves. Just like us. Remarkably, amazingly and delightfully, these people are the people God uses. The disappointed ones. Sneaky and snarly people who often acted before they thought, who failed to act when they should have and sometimes didn't act at all.

Yet they were called friends of God. The man who named the people of Israel, Jacob, was a mama's boy. The one who became brave enough to stand up to his wealthy adopted family and side with the oppressed immigrant workers, Moses, lived with a stubborn insecurity. Rahab, a woman whose circumstances led to her prostituting herself, became the one who helped establish a country for the "pure and holy" people of God. King David, famous for his devotion to God, gave into his voracious sexual appetites and passion.

These are the ones God calls friends: people like the great prophet Elijah who struggled with depression, fear and a weird streak of pride that caused him to do an ugly power play over the fate of two little boys. Jonah, the prophet to the ancient city of Nineveh, who didn't want to go because of his racism. John the Baptist, who would today likely be holed up in Idaho somewhere, living off his produce and writing treatises against the government and church.

If you're ready for a bigger life and to live in a world of tension and transformation, you have to find people like this bunch because they are the friends of God. Sometimes awkward, occasionally irrational and always deeply flawed, these are the people God chooses.

We forget that God doesn't choose people because of their capacity for greatness or because of their ability to operate within their comfort zone. God chooses people who are willing to risk their necks to share what they have been given, people who have been so amazed at being chosen, so aware of the gift, of their indebtedness that they are willing to do anything to live it out.

God chooses to bestow grace on the graceless, love on the loveless. God gives a name to those who had no name. And God tells an utterly forgettable tribe of wandering nomads that they are "the chosen ones." Does that sound at all like you?

Jesus Believes in You

Former British prime minister Tony Blair spoke at the 2009 National Day of Prayer Breakfast in Washington, DC. Blair grew up in a nominally Anglican household that didn't think much about God. The family went to church Christmas Eve and Easter, but beyond that, there wasn't much talk about God.

Blair's understanding of God changed when he was nine years old. His dad had suffered a stroke and was near death. His mother sent young Tony to school, hoping to help him keep a semblance of normalcy. While at school, his teacher knelt to pray with him.

Nine-year-old Tony sadly cautioned his teacher, "I'm afraid my father doesn't believe in God."

"That doesn't matter," his teacher replied without missing a beat, "God believes in him."[2]

Imagine what this meant to the young boy nervously waiting to hear whether his father might live or die: "God believes in him." Blair said his love for God began then and there. *God believes in you* and there's nothing you can do that will change that fact. God believes in you. Saying that makes something shift inside of me. Somehow the mountains start to look a lot more manageable to me, and I start to see a way that perhaps I could cross that sea on dry land.

Fyodor Dostoyevsky's book *The Brothers Karamazov* is a delightful Russian novel about faith and the loss of it. One memorable scene is the chapter titled "The Grand Inquisitor."[3] A Spanish cardinal comes across Christ on the steps of the Seville Cathedral during the Spanish Inquisition, and Christ is doing what Christ does: restoring sight to an old man, bringing a little girl back from the dead. The common people have not made the connection that this strange, compelling miracle worker is Jesus himself. But the cardinal realizes it in a flash, immediately grasping the implications of what it would mean for the church if this sort of activity is allowed to continue. Jesus is quickly arrested and after a sham trial is sentenced to be burned at the stake the following day.

But late that night the cardinal visits Jesus in his cell. He must tell Jesus all the mistakes and missteps he believes Jesus made during his time on earth. "You could have demanded people love you—forced them to not have a choice, and instead you offered them the very thing they are incapable of handling: *freedom*. We killed you once for that, and we will do so again."

Why does Jesus come back? Why does God continue to bother with us? Why would Jesus want to continue to engage with us?

There are several answers, I think. The apostle John might have answered that it's simply the very nature of God. God is love (1 John 4:8). And John knew something about this. Sharp-eyed readers of Scripture know that John likely never even used his personal name in his Gospel narrative. He just referred to himself as the "one whom the Lord loved." John's very identity was only found in Jesus' love for him.

There is this persistent recklessness to God that Jesus often talked about. Christ completely reframes the exalted, transcendent and mysterious Jehovah by describing the Father as a grieved dad who hikes up his robe and rushes across the field to embrace a long lost son. Or as a shepherd who spends all night outside, searching for the one sheep lost on the mountainside.

This is the nature of God, Jesus says. And this relentless pursuit by God still continues. Some of you have felt this.

We don't really know how to talk about it:

The universe is trying to tell me something, we say.

Or, *I just had this feeling about what I was supposed to do.*

The writer Anne Lamott describes this tenacity of God in a memorable fashion. Lamott is a San Francisco, liberal-leaning, dreadlock-wearing, single mother, aging hippie writer with a colorful past.

Several years ago she also began to follow Jesus. It began when she sensed this presence that she couldn't shake.

I knew beyond any doubt that it was Jesus. I felt him as surely as I feel my dog lying nearby as I write this.

And I was appalled. I thought about my life and my brilliant hilarious progressive friends. I thought about what everyone would think of me if I became a Christian and it seemed an utterly impossible thing that simply could not be allowed to happen. I turned to the wall and said out loud, "I would rather die." . . .

But then everywhere I went I had the feeling that a little cat was following me, wanting me to reach down and pick it up, wanting me to open the door and let it in. But I knew what would happen. You let a cat in one time, give it a little milk, and then it stays forever. So I tried to keep one step ahead of it, slamming my houseboat door when I entered or left.

And one week later, when I went back to church, I was so hung-over I couldn't stand up for the songs, and this time I stayed for the sermon, which I thought was so ridiculous, like someone trying to convince me of the existence of extraterrestrials, but the last song was so deep and raw and pure that I could not escape. . . . I opened up to that feeling and it washed over me.

I began to cry and left before the benediction, and I raced home and felt the little cat running along at my heels, and when I walked down the dock past dozens of potted flowers, under a sky as blue as one of God's own dreams, and opened the door to my houseboat, and I stood there a minute, and then I hung my head and said: "F— it. I quit." I took a long deep breath and said out loud, "All right. You can come in."

So this was my beautiful moment of conversion.[4]

In an earlier age, the late 1800s, another writer, poet Francis Thompson, described Lamott's cat as the "Hound of Heaven," one whom the poet resisted at every turn:

I fled Him, down the nights and down the days;
I fled Him, down the arches of the years;

I fled Him, down the labyrinthine ways
   Of my own mind; and in the midst of tears
I hid from Him, and under running laughter.
     Up vistaed hopes I sped.[5]

God is still pursuing the world. You. Me. All of us.

You know that sense of certainty that sweeps over you at the sight of a magnificent sunrise, this pervading sense of goodness of the earth? Or that moment when your wrong was suddenly met with forgiveness. Or how, when you're fearful or alone, there is, on occasion, this deep sense that you're being held up by some unseen force, some comforting power?

Can these be nudges, whispers, little pokes, pointers to a reality that there's more here than what you first thought?

God is relentless at courting us with grace. Even killing God won't keep God away from those he loves. That includes you—who has picked up this book with suspicion, and you—who left any formal faith years ago. It includes the child you may have had baptized in some superstitious grip, and it includes the weathered, weary skeptic.

The embrace of Jesus on the cross was specifically for sinners—people who have been separated from each other and from the experience of God. It was for people who, at best, only had a passing sense of God's glory in their midst. And the resurrection came first to those who had denied, abandoned and doubted Jesus. *Especially them.*

I remember meeting Michelle at a particularly vulnerable spot in her life. Her father was dying of cancer. She believed in God, but she didn't *believe enough*, she thought. Her big worry was that God was not paying attention to her declining father's condition because his daughter, Michelle, didn't have enough faith.

We're at the coffee shop just down the street from our church, and this thirtysomething woman is sobbing into her drink, wracked by the guilt that her lack of faith was preventing her father from getting well. I reached over and grabbed her hand and said, "I don't know if this is going to be good news or bad news for you. But you are simply not powerful enough to stop God from loving your dad."

Among Jesus' first followers, shame was not powerful enough to stop Jesus from returning to Peter. Doubt was not strong enough to keep Jesus away from Thomas. Grief wasn't thick enough to prevent Jesus' tenderness from reaching Mary.

None of these human conditions were powerful enough to stop the resurrected Jesus from showing up. Peter, Thomas and Mary were not powerful enough. And you know what? You're not either. The Grand Inquisitor story didn't end with Christ being burned at the stake for blasphemy. No, after the Inquisitor—the cardinal— stopped speaking, he waited some time for his prisoner to answer him. "His silence weighed down upon him. He saw that the Prisoner had listened intently all the time, looking gently in his face and evidently not wishing to reply. The old man longed for him to say something, however bitter and terrible." But instead, the prisoner suddenly approached the old man in silence and softly kissed him on his bloodless aged lips. That was all he answered. The old man shuddered. He went to the door, opened it, and said to him, "Go, and never, never come again."

It is we who opt out, not Jesus.

Coming undone can be the best thing that ever happens to us, if we let it be. Jesus said, "Listen! I am standing at the door, knocking; if you hear my voice and open the door, I will come in to you and eat with you, and you with me" (Revelation 3:20). The Son of God says this in some of the last pages of the last book in the Bible. But it's the same offer God put on the table many, many thousands of years earlier, back in the Garden of Eden when men and women were created to be image bearers of God.

All of the parts of your past—go ahead and name them: adulterer, liar, cheater, user, abuser, hypocrite, snob. And all the adjectives that may go with those nouns: sneaky, devious, duplicitous, selfish and cowardly—go ahead and name them too. But at the same time name all the other things God says about you: Name the fact that you are marked with the blessing of God, called the son, the daughter, of the Lord Most High. Remember the fact that you are endowed with the capacity to create, to forgive, to redeem and to love freely—all divine. Remember the truth that you are more powerful that you can imagine and more fragile than you think and that *everyone else around you is as well*.

Remember that God always beckons us into the larger world of life. Calling us into the people we were created to be.

God keeps urging, *You don't have to live like this! Let me love you. Let* love *love you*.

There is only love. There has only ever been love. And there only ever will be love. And that love believes in you.

Acknowledgments

*I*nterdependence is woven throughout this book. This project would not have seen the light of day without the steadfast support of Peg Paugh—her contributions of scheduling, editing, proofing and encouraging cannot be overstated. Peg's belief in this project gave me hope. I cannont thank her enough. Thanks also to the friends at LaSalle who read and wrote thoughtful questions: Susan Schaefer and Amber Johnson, Linda Weinberg and my colleague Oreon Trickey.

LaSalle Street Church is filled with quiet heroes—people who struggle to live authentically and to love generously. They have opened up their lives and allowed me to be present at some of their most vulnerable moments. Together we have celebrated births and grieved at bedsides; we have rejoiced at reunited sons and mourned the loss of marriages. We have lived life together, each day rising to meet the love of God and the face of our neighbor. I'm thankful to be among their company.

Anyone who has had a child knows that your heart almost explodes with love when you see them for the first time. My heart continues to explode when I think of my children: Sumner, Porter and Burnley. And a big thank you to my husband, Terry. The man my mother always said was "one in 10 million."

She was right.

Notes

1 Coming Undone: The Best Worst Day of My Life
[1] Thomas Stearns Eliot, "The Love Song of J. Alfred Prufrock," in *Prufrock and Other Observations* (New York: A. A. Knopf, 1920), p. 5.

2 Broken Relationships and the Beginning of Emptiness
[1] Annie Dillard, *Pilgrim at Tinker Creek* (New York: Harper Perennial, 1988), p. 9.
[2] Scott Cairns, "The Entrance of Sin," in *Philokalia* (Lincoln, NE: Zoo Press, 2002), p. 117.
[3] Robert Frost, "Death of the Hired Man," in *North of Boston* (New York: Henry Holt, 1915), p 14.
[4] Thanks to Barbara Brown Taylor for her analysis of sin in *Speaking of Sin: The Lost Language of Salvation* (Cambridge, MA: Cowley, 2000).
[5] Marianne Williamson, *Return to Love* (New York: HarperCollins, 1992), p. 165.
[6] John Milton, "Samson Agonistes," in *The Complete Poems of John Milton* (New York: P. F. Collier, 1909-1914).

3 Wanting More, Finding Less
[1] Luke 6:24; Luke 16:13; Matthew 6:19; Matthew 19:24; Luke 6:30; Mark 10:21; Luke 12:13-21, my paraphrase.

4 Hiding Behind Masks
[1] See Jodi Wilgoren, "College Suspends Professor for Vietnam Fabrications," *New York Times*, August 18, 2001, www.nytimes.com/2001/08/18/us/college-suspends-professor-for-vietnam-fabrications.html.
[2] Ibid.
[3] Daniel Goleman, *Vital Lies, Simple Truths: The Psychology of Self-Deception* (New York: Bloomsbury, 1998).
[4] Benjamin Zander and Rosamund Stone Zander, *The Art of Possibility* (Cambridge, MA: Harvard Business Press, 2000).

[5]See Shane's webpage at the Simple Way website, www.thesimpleway.org/shane.
[6]For a fuller treatment on the theological concept of sloth, see Rebecca Konyndyk DeYoung, *Glittering Vices: A New Look at the Seven Deadly Sins and Their Remedies* (Grand Rapids: Brazos Press, 2009).

5 Behind the Mask

[1]Leonard Cohen, "Anthem," in *The Future*, Stranger Music, 1992. Used by permission.
[2]Julian of Norwich, *Revelations of Divine Love*. Quoted in a devotional from Church of Our Savior, Washington, DC.

6 Transforming Fear

[1]Anne Lamott, *Traveling Mercies: Some Thoughts on Faith* (New York: Random House, 1999), p. 117.
[2]See, for example, Bruce Goldstein, *Cognitive Psychology: Connecting Mind, Research, and Everyday Experience* (Belmont, CA: Wadsworth Cengage Learning, 2011), chap. 7; James M. Lampinen, Jeffrey S. Neuschatz and Andrew D. Cling, *The Psychology of Eyewitness Identification* (New York: Psychology Press, 2012).
[3]"What have you to do with me, Jesus, Son of the Most High God? I adjure you by God, do not torment me" (Mark 5:7).
[4]Richard Rohr, *Everything Belongs: The Gift of Contemplative Prayer* (New York: Crossroad, 1999), pp. 19-20.

7 The Risk of Trust

[1]Frederick Buechner, *Peculiar Treasures* (San Francisco: Harper San Francisco, 1993), p. 39.

8 The Reward of Trust

[1]Rainer Maria Rilke, "The Man Watching," in *Selected Poems of Rainer Maria Rilke*, ed. Robert Bly (New York: Harper & Row, 1981), p. 105.
[2]Percy Bysshe Shelley, "Ozymandias," in *Rosalind and Helen, a Modern Eclogue, with Other Poems* (London: Ollier, 1819).

10 Childlike Trust

[1]Roald Dahl, *George's Marvelous Medicine* (New York: Knopf, 1981).
[2]Gordon MacKenzie, *Orbiting the Giant Hairball: A Corporate Fool's Guide to Surviving with Grace* (New York: Penguin, 1998).
[3]Tony Campolo, *Let Me Tell You a Story* (Nashville: Word, 2000), p. 12.
[4]Tony Campolo, "If I Should Wake Before I Die," episode 3627 of *30 Good*

Minutes, a production of the Chicago Sunday Evening Club. First broadcast on April 25, 1993.
[5]Ibid.

11 Restoring Your Identity
[1]John Steinbeck, *East of Eden* (New York: Penguin, 2002), p. 302.
[2]Private email correspondence with the author. Used by permission.
[3]Irenaeus, quoted in *Catechism of the Catholic Church* (New York: Doubleday), p. 719.

12 Imagine Love
[1]Nancy Gibbs and Michael Duffy, *The Preacher and the Presidents: Billy Graham in the White House* (New York: Center Street, 2007).

13 Community: The Third Way
[1]Martin Buber, *I and Thou*, trans. Walter Arnold Kauffman (New York: Scribner, 1970).
[2]Tertullian, quoted in Skip Heitzig, *When God Prays* (Wheaton, IL: Tyndale House, 2003), p. 146.

14 Little Choices: It's All Little Choices
[1]Ernest Becker, *The Denial of Death* (New York: Free Press, 1973), pp. 26, 51.

15 The Arc of the Future
[1]C. S. Lewis, *Weight of Glory* (New York: HarperOne, 1980), p. 46.
[2]Tony Blair, "Full text of Tony Blair's Speech to the National Prayer Breakfast," *The Office of Tony Blair*, February 5, 2009, www.tonyblairoffice.org/speeches/entry/full-text-of-tony-blairs-speech-to-the-national-prayer-breakfast.
[3]Fyodor Dostoyevsky, "The Grand Inquisitor," in *The Brothers Karamazov* (New York: Macmillan, 1922), pp. 259-79.
[4]Anne Lamott, *Traveling Mercies* (New York: Random House, 1999), pp. 49-50.
[5]Francis Thompson, "The Hound of Heaven," in *Poems: Works of Francis Thompson, Part 1* (Whitefish, MT: Kessinger, 2003), p. 107.

Questions for Reflection or Discussion

Chapter One: Coming Undone

1. Laura talks about the experience of becoming undone, saying it was both the worst and best day of her life. Realizing the growth and good that has come through a difficult or humbling experience usually requires the perspective of time.

   Think through your experiences to a time that seemed awful but led you to a breakthrough. Share this story with a friend or journal about it.

2. Was there ever a loss or failure in your life that elicited a sense of relief? How long did it take you to appreciate this freedom?

3. Laura tells of excessively eating coffee cake and drinking wine on the day of her divorce. How were these excesses also a communion for her? Where have you found grace or comfort in unexpected places and untraditional means?

4. Laura writes that what appear to be kindness, openness and vulnerability can sometimes truly be pride, power and self-containment. Do you believe that is true for you? How do you mask your true thoughts with more socially acceptable attitudes? In what circumstances are you more likely to do this?

5. Even in the midst of lies, deceptions and falsehoods, Laura writes that she and others have a persistent sense that they are created for

higher and better things. Do you feel this as well? If so, what causes you to believe this?

Chapter Two: Broken Relationships

1. The Hebrews understood that everything that is created is good, but soon after creation it begins to fray. Do you feel this sense of fraying in your own life? Think of two or three of your most intimate relationships. Can you identify areas where there may be some fraying?

2. Have you ever felt truly at home, at a place where you were loved and valued and supported no matter what? How can you create that sort of environment for others? What sort of "fraying" makes this difficult for you?

3. Consider your actions or words of the past week. Can you identify words or actions of deceit you may have said or done? What could have happened if you had been more truthful?

4. Samson's gifts had a shadow side. What are your greatest gifts? Can you identify some of their shadow sides? What have been some of their consequences?

5. *Chatah* is the Hebrew word for the aspect of sin encompassing the risks we didn't take, the fear that stops us from loving or hoping. How have you experienced the sin of *chatah?* What bold steps would you take if you weren't afraid? What would you need to believe about God and about yourself to make this possible?

Chapter Three: Wanting More, Finding Less

1. Have you ever known in your gut that something is wrong long before you were able to explain it? How did you know? What were the signs?

2. What is that "10% more" that you desire? Have you ever had the

experience of getting what you want and then finding it "not enough"?

3. Make a quick list of 5-10 times you can recall being truly happy. What do these times have in common?

4. What is the one thing you don't want to give up? Is there anything you want too much to allow yourself to have? Are there any consequences of these desires?

Chapter Four: Hiding Behind Masks

1. How do you feel when you suspect others are judging you? Do you grow embarrassed? Lash out in anger? Become defensive? What productive ways have you found to counteract these feelings?

2. Consider the situation of author/professor Joseph Ellis and the story he eventually took on as his truth. In a similar fashion, others can tell stories about us that we take on as our truths (a parent may have called you "stupid"; classmates may have called you "ugly" or "fat"). What stories have you taken on as being your truth?

3. There's a fine line between hoping to be your best self, and allowing yourself to receive grace when you miss the mark. Laura says it is deception to wrap yourself in an appearance of perfection, when in reality you feel you are in shambles. Have you ever sensed someone was trying to appear perfect when in reality they were struggling? What gave it away? What are you afraid others will realize about you?

4. Laura writes that your identity as a child of God is not a challenge to live up to, but a promise to live into. Take a minute to dwell on that idea. If you truly and deeply believed this, how would it change your thoughts? Your prayers? Your hopes and dreams? Your daily life? What freedom would this give you?

5. Laura defines sloth as "purposeless activity" and a "disordered attachment." How can slothfulness be remedied by love?

6. Think for a minute about the difference between sloth and Shalom. If the two are opposite points on a spectrum, where on that spectrum does your life lie? What changes to your schedule, to your sense of purpose, would you need to move just a little closer to Shalom?

Chapter Five: Behind the Mask

1. What are some of the masks you wear? What are the fears that led to that mask's construction?

2. While Lot's story provides an extreme example of fears feeding greed, we can often find examples in our fears feeding a false sense of need. Can you think of an example from your own life? How have you seen this develop over time? What are the indications that your "needs" are driven by fear rather than a reality that is grounded in Shalom?

3. The message of this chapter is that you don't have to be above average. God is more gentle with us than we are with others. Do you believe that? Where could you be more gentle with your self and with others?

Chapter Six: Transforming Fear

1. So many of the stories Jesus told, or that are recorded about Jesus, involve people who are faced with a choice: leave a past of fear and uncertainty, and choose a better, more hopeful future. Some, like the woman at the well, are able to make that choice. Others, like the rich young ruler, go away sad. What do you think holds people back from choosing a better future? Is it circumstances? Their own beliefs about themselves and what they deserve or are

capable of? A lack of humility? A lack of vision?

2. Laura states we often see only what we expect to see. If so, there is a range of experiences that we miss. How can you improve your vision of all life presents to you?

3. In Anne Lamott's story, the rescued man in the bar failed to identify the divine intervention of the Eskimos who saved him. Who have been the Eskimos in your life? Could you imagine their appearance relates to a larger story of your life?

4. Have you ever avoided the living water for fear of its danger?

5. Spend a few moments examining your life. What constitutes the center of your life? What defines the circumference? Do you run the risk of mistaking the circumstances of life as reality?

6. What truths would you have to be honest about in order to move closer to the center of your life?

Chapter Seven: The Risk of Trust

1. Having the faith to walk on water, figuratively, is not just about your own spiritual journey. It's also about the contribution you're then able to make for the world. How do you see yourself fitting into a bigger story?

2. Where do you find yourself looking up and asking, "Hey! I could use a little help down here!"

3. How can your own inward focus make you estranged from others around you? What uncomfortable complexities would you face if you attempted to connect more deeply and honestly with others?

4. Have you had moments in your life where your "little steps of faith" have led to unexpectedly large results?

5. Where do you need to dive into the water today? How safe is your boat?

Chapter Eight: The Reward of Trust

1. "To trust in God isn't to be assured of success. It is a promise that we can commit ourselves to something great, and in so doing, we can experience something powerfully both human and divine in the process of that commitment." Have you ever equated trust in God with the assurance of success? What have you learned instead? How would you explain this to a friend struggling to understand a failure or seemingly unanswered prayer?

2. Laura uses the Rilke poem "The Man Watching" to discuss winning by losing. How is it possible to grow by being "defeated decisively" by a Greater Being?

3. God isn't looking for perfection, God is looking for people willing to engage. Do you believe this? Why or why not? If it is true, what does it mean for your life? Your church?

4. Consider Laura's statement that we will not change "until the pain of staying as you are is greater than the pain of changing." Do you believe that? Can you identify examples in your own life where that happened?

5. God had to call Samuel to stop grieving the past and begin to take action for the future. We are often the same way, seeing the need for change but locked in a cycle of inertia that allows us to blame others, or not face the deep changes we need in ourselves. Can you think of a time in your life when you successfully fought inertia? What made you ready to change? What happened afterward? How did you feel about yourself? Your faith?

6. Laura writes about "patching on" the trappings of Christianity and religious practice, but missing the true meaning. Take stock of your own spiritual practices: Are you connecting with the real meaning of each one? Are you going through routines or entering into a place of worship?

Chapter Nine: What Does God Want from Me?

1. If God isn't watching us like "babysitters on a nanny-cam," how is God watching us? What does this divine connection with us look like?

2. Laura distinguishes between the "primary message of God" with the "ways and means" of Christianity. In what ways do the "ways and means" assist in living the Christian life? How can they be misused?

3. Laura says self-loathing ranges from recklessness to ascetic self-denial. Where do you fall between these two extremes? What might God actually want for you?

4. Consider Jesus' words to "abide in me as I abide in you." Is this a conditional promise that can only be fulfilled if you do your part?

5. The presence of God, Laura writes, is seen only in random gasps of recognition and wonder. Think of a few big moments in your life where you've had these gasps. Now think of a few small moments, today even, when you've had quiet recognitions and small glimpses of wonder. How do you see God in these gasps?

6. We often fear that our faith will be made weaker by our failures, but Peter's faith was deepened after he betrayed Christ. How have you grown through failure?

Chapter Ten: Childlike Trust

1. Do you have the in-the-moment confidence of a child? What one thing could you do today to be more childlike?

2. "Living in the moment" has become a buzz-phrase. But the truth of it isn't dimmed by overuse. Are there some patterns or windows of time where you are able to better "live in the moment" than others? What distinguishes those moments? Are

there practices you could intentionally put in place to make them more frequent?

3. If you are a parent, how do you deal with a sense of inadequacy?

4. The Trinity reminds us that God's essence is located in community. How does the community around you reflect God's essence? How do you contribute to that reflection?

5. Describe ways in which childlike living can help restore your identity.

Chapter Eleven: Restoring Your identity

1. Recall the story of Lois, walking out of her way to take a birthday card and treats to a homeless man, as a testimony to his value and worth. What similar action could you take today to remind someone around you of his (or her) value and worth as an individual created in the image of God?

2. John the Baptist was interested in people chopping down the false trees of their lives. What religious trees of yours would have to come down if you were going to begin a new relationship with God?

3. *Metanoia* is the point at which you determine to make a fresh start. A U-turn. It's easy to make the decision, and even easier to lose your resolve. Do you have a sense for what changes you would like to make in your life? How will you steel your resolve?

4. We often shirk from uncomfortable circumstances and undesirable responsibilities, like Tyson longed to leave his lifeguarding job behind. Tyson realized, eventually, that he was in his role for a reason, and his attitude toward it was important, even life-giving. Are you in a challenging circumstance? What thoughts and prayers are shaping your attitude toward this position?

Chapter Twelve: Imagine Love

1. Have you ever received unconditional love from another human being? Have you ever given it? How did it make you feel and act?

2. Identify some segments of people with whom you don't associate. What would it take to reach out to them? What prevents you from doing so?

3. Laura talks about a group of people gathered at the Jordan River, people coming from all walks of life but united by a single desire: they wanted something better. Many of us feel this longing for our lives. Do you? What "better" do you want? What is the root cause of this desire?

4. Being near true power can be intoxicating. It can also cause us to lose our way, to begin to behave in ways that are not our best self. Can you think of a time you've used power to belittle or undermine others? When you've failed to stand up to the misuse of power around you? Can you think of a time you have? What gave you the courage in that circumstance that you lacked in other circumstances?

Chapter Thirteen: Community

1. Laura says the cross runs against the grain of some of our American posturing about independence. Do you agree or disagree? Why?

2. "The cross of Jesus takes an assertive, almost downright aggressive stance in the direction of others." If this is the direction of the cross, does your church reflect this? Your family? Where do you see this other-orientation best lived out?

3. How would you live your life differently if you "held" onto things loosely?

4. We've all had the experience of "drawing a line in the sand." Why

did you draw them? Have the lines you've drawn been useful to the community? Out of reverence for God and humility toward others? Are there lines you're drawing now?

5. The *Third Way* concept requires each of us to lean in toward others, trusting along the way. Take a minute to imagine your life, fully lived in this third way. What would be the same? What would change? What's one small step you could take today to move in this direction?

6. Reflect on the Quaker story and the premise that we are all called to engage in different ways at different times. Can you recall times when you were called to something and refused the call? Or times when you engaged for other reasons even though you weren't called? Were there differences in the outcome? What are you being called to at this point in time?

Chapter Fourteen: Little Choices

1. A near-death experience gave Laura the perspective that small decisions, when made out of fear, can keep us from the future God desires for us, while small steps of faithfulness can slowly lead us in surprising new directions. It's the smallest of choices that move us forward or backward. What principles do you want governing your small (and big) choices? Draft a short list of three or four guiding principles; post it somewhere prominent and meditate on them for a few weeks until you're sure you have the right principles as your guide. Then discuss these ideas with a few trusted others.

2. Are you someone who feels settled? Or someone for whom life seems unpredictable? How could you welcome change and look for growth? How could you welcome stability and look for maturity?

Chapter Fifteen: The Arc of the Future

1. When we're busy it's easy to stay on "autopilot," moving mechanically through our days without awareness of the grace around us. Spend the next few hours of your day "off autopilot." Consciously think about each decision you make, each bite of food you take, each conversation you have. What have you noticed that you might have otherwise missed? How could you carry this awareness into the future?

2. Moving forward, living interdependently, necessitates friction. How has the friction of growth, or the friction of relationships and community, shaped you into something more like Christ? How does your attitude toward your current circumstances change when you see them as part of being shaped and remade?

3. What does it mean to know *God believes in you*? Is it frightening? Nonsensical? Is there anything about that phrase powerfully liberating to you?

COURAGE. CONFIDENCE. CALLING.

Some voices challenge us. Others support or encourage us. Voices can move us to change our minds, draw close to God, discover a new spiritual gift. The voices of others are shaping who we are.

The voices behind IVP Crescendo join together to draw us into God's story. We'll discover God's work around the globe even as we learn to love the people around the corner. We'll have opportunity to heal our places of pain. We'll discover new ways to love our families. We'll hear God's voice speaking into our lives as we discover new places of influence.

IVP Crescendo invites you to join in the rising chorus

- *to listen to the voices of others*
- *to hear the voice of God*
- *and to grow your own voice in*

COURAGE. CONFIDENCE. CALLING.

ivpress.com/crescendo
ivpress.com/crescendo-social